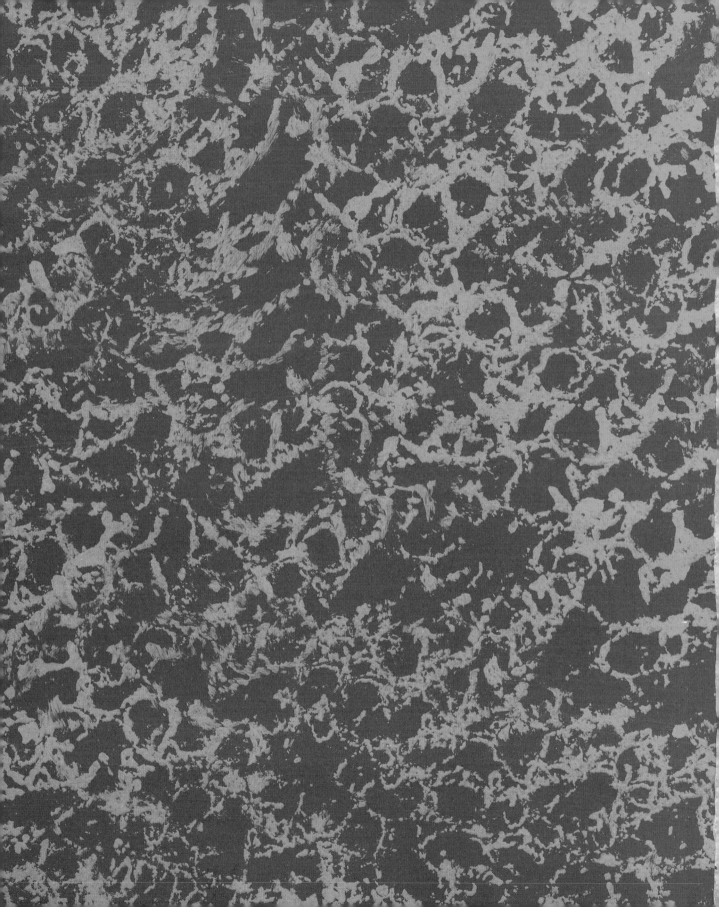

COUNTRY FINISHES

COUNTRY FINISHES

SIMPLE PAINT TREATMENTS
for FOUND *and* UNFINISHED FURNITURE

RICHARD KOLLATH

PHOTOGRAPHS BY GEORGE ROSS

A BULFINCH PRESS BOOK
LITTLE, BROWN AND COMPANY
BOSTON NEW YORK TORONTO LONDON

FIRST EDITION

Library of Congress
Cataloging-in-Publication Data
Kollath, Richard.
Country finishes:
simple paint treatments for found and unfinished furniture
Richard Kollath; photographs by George Ross.
p.   cm.
"A Bulfinch Press book."
Includes index.
ISBN 0-8212-1994-4
1. Furniture finishing.   2. Country furniture.   I. Title.
TT199.4.K65 1993
684.1'043 — dc20 92-45280

10   9   8   7   6   5   4   3   2   1

Bulfinch Press is an imprint and trademark of Little, Brown and Company (Inc.)
Published simultaneously in Canada by Little, Brown & Company (Canada) Limited

PRINTED IN SINGAPORE

I dedicate this book to my good friend Paul Girolamo,
with love and gratitude for the joy his friendship has brought to my life.

TABLE *of* CONTENTS

In the Hudson River Valley, where I live, the countryside is dotted with dozens of antique shops housed in old barns. There are, of course, many antique businesses in traditional stores; but there's just something about those barns I get excited about. When I am driving down the road, their familiar signs are like beacons to me, and I find myself heading for those open doors. All of these shops share certain unifying characteristics: piles of objects, irregular passageways, and poor light. They all seem to have dark corners where you have to spend a moment allowing your eyes to adjust. These barns and businesses radiate mystery and adventure.

For many people, the whole process of finding and refinishing furniture is a welcomed activity. Somehow the work entailed dissolves, leaving simple satisfaction and pride of accomplishment. What I have always found most rewarding is the sense of the hunt — the actual discovery of a piece of furniture, the aesthetic reaction that captures my senses and beckons me to purchase it, to claim it and then reclaim it. For me, this adventure began in my childhood.

There was an old barn on the property where I grew up, a small, classically proportioned structure with a wide double door on one end. When that door was opened, long shafts of light flooded the usually dim interior. The floor of the barn was covered with hundreds of clay flowerpots in graduated sizes that my father had stored there. There were shelves filled with old boxes whose contents echoed the past.

Those boxes were always in shadow. It was a place that contained both adventure and mystery and held my fascination and interest when I was a young boy. I played in this space and explored each corner until everything became familiar.

Above the main room was an attic or hayloft that could only be reached by a ladder attached to an interior side wall of the barn. Climbing it was easy, but there was no toehold at the top, so the stretch to bridge the expanse of the square opening to set foot on the attic floor was at first very frightening and nearly impossible. In time I conquered it, and my reward was an amazing discovery: a treasury of old headboards, picture frames, tables, and two Boston rockers. Each rocker was covered with multiple coats of enamel paint, the last of which was black. There was something about them that fascinated me — their proportion and design, the juxtaposition of the long rungs on the seat back and heavy cap on the top, the arc of the runners and the cane of the seat. These two rockers soon became a part of my summer and my life.

My father helped me lower the rockers from the hayloft to the ground with a rope, and together we set up a work area in the shade of a great maple tree. I remember my first paint-stripping experience as a solitary one, and it seemed I spent the entire summer sanding, scrubbing, scraping, and rubbing, eventually using a fine steel wool until the wood was smooth and clear. Both my parents added encouragement during each messy stage of the refinishing, and my mother recaned the seats. Once the chairs were stripped and stained they were absolutely beautiful. They were brought into our home and over the years provided each of us with countless rides into our own worlds of dreams, into sweet summer naps and winter readings.

I suspect I experienced a bit of magic that summer. That early childhood experience became a seed of inspiration for me, and refinishing furniture has provided an enormous degree of pleasure and pride throughout my life. The world I discovered is still there, waiting for you to discover for yourself.

Country Finishes is a product of the talents, efforts, and absolute good will of many friends and associates. It is with deep appreciation that I acknowledge the individual contributions of:

Emma Sweeney of Curtis Brown, Ltd., for your support in working out all the essential details.

Lindley Boegehold of Bulfinch Press, for your enthusiasm and your guidance and important insights throughout the development of this book.

Edward McCann, friend and partner, for lending the text of this book its clarity; I thank you for your contributions and support on every level and at every phase of this project.

George Ross, for your absolutely beautiful photographs, the result of great patience and a strong visual sensitivity; working with you is a genuine pleasure.

Virginia Edwards, for your aesthetic talents and design skills; your subtle contributions make this book a treat for the eyes.

Kevin Moore, for lending your technical expertise to the photographic process, as well as delighting us all with your wry wit.

Stephanne Pleshette-McCann, for all your support, and for preparing an endless flow of delicious meals.

John and Ruth Kollath, my parents, for your continuous encouragement, and for providing throughout my life many opportunities to explore and expand.

Bert and Didi Carpenter, for helping me search throughout the North Carolina landscape for furniture and other objects, sharing with me the joy of the hunt.

I wish also to thank the friends who generously allowed me to photograph their homes; I very much appreciated their cheerful tolerance of the periodic disruption to their lives and routines: Paco and Sara Trilla, Jay Halpern, Gregory Newham, Fred Misner, Bob Palmatier, Edward and Stephanne McCann.

COUNTRY FINISHES

Country Finishes is a comprehensive, step-by-step guide to the application of creative painted treatments on found furniture and decorative accessories. It is a treasure book of simple, direct projects that you can do in a weekend or short period of time, within your home and within your budget.

This book contains twenty-two projects incorporating eleven fully illustrated techniques. You'll find projects and techniques designed to give your old furniture a new strength and richness using color, pattern, texture, and original design.

Country Finishes will provide you with many contented, creative hours. Each project in this book will allow you opportunities to repeat various techniques or processes, beginning with the fundamentals of stripping and preparing the piece for painting. This is a book to have fun with, to enhance and enrich your home decoration, and to bring you a sense of satisfaction and pride. What *Country Finishes* will establish for you is a sequential structure to follow when creating specific painted treatments. Following the examples in this book, you can bring new life to attic relics, hand-me-downs, tag sale finds, and other neglected pieces, as well as new unfinished furniture. From an interior design standpoint, the nineties are being defined as less pretentious, with a strong emphasis on an eclectic mix of fur-

nishings and materials. The treatments you will learn in this book are sure to complement and enhance your environment.

This book has been designed to provide you with a series of separate techniques, all of which build upon each other to produce many variations of surface treatments. With the understanding of the basic step-by-step processes, you will personally be able to select furniture and create your own treasures. This is a ticket to your own country finish creativity.

In one sense, this book is also about an appreciation of history. Many of us desire a tie to our heritage, a link to our past. You may have a hand-me-down piece of family furniture, perhaps not something really special, but something whose sentimental value makes you want to incorporate it into the overall design of your home. You may finally have acquired your father's old secretary desk or that great quirky table you've wanted from your grandmother, but because of the condition it's in, it doesn't comfortably relate to your environment.

You may be seeking to change or update your decor, but because of space or financial limitations, you realize changes must come through looking at what you presently own in a new way. With a change of skin, a change of color, that old piece can suddenly adopt a new character that will allow it to unify a room or stand on its own. Almost every element in your rooms can be held up for scrutiny, and each piece of furniture has its own inherent potential.

Most of the surface treatments in this book reflect a certain coziness. There's a warmth and richness that comes from having a piece of painted furniture within your home. Painted furniture is familiar and comfortable, like your favorite pair of old blue jeans, with gentle surfaces and soft patinas. These pieces have a character all their own — a certain spirit that blends beautifully with highly polished wood furniture. Painted pieces become part of the cadence of a room, and part of the cadence of your life. They add a new rhythm and harmony to the standard configurations of a home outfitted with what have come to be viewed as more traditional home furnishings. A piece of painted furniture can be the poetic element of your interior space.

There are many ways to acquire quality affordable furniture suitable for refinishing. Traditionally, people used to simply inherit furniture as it was passed down through the family. Today, we scour antique stores, garage and tag sales, flea markets, consignment shops, auctions and estate sales. Many chain stores around the country now offer ready-made unfinished furniture at a reasonable price — a boon to those who want to buy a piece of new unfinished furniture to complement their environment. People who just want a change can also work with the furnishings they have on hand. In general, people are more conscious of economic and environmental considerations today, and enjoy the satisfaction that only comes from doing it themselves.

There are a number of new environmentally friendly refinishing products on the market that enable the apartment dweller to strip and finish furniture indoors without fear of hazardous chemicals. Whether you bring a piece to refinish into your basement, your garage, or your kitchen, all the projects in this book can be done in whatever space you have available. If you can accommodate the piece within your home, you can give it a new finish within your home as well.

Each of these projects has been created in such a way that anyone can do it. This book is the resource that will help you refinish that strange little table you have tucked away in your attic; perhaps it's the right proportion but the wrong finish. Start by experimenting on small-scale objects like boxes, chairs, and that little table to become familiar with the various processes, using the ones that are most interesting to you. From that starting point, take on a larger challenge, expanding your painting techniques, and go for that antique dresser in your bedroom or the unfinished entertainment center in the family room. As your skills and confidence increase, you'll be able to tackle larger projects, combining techniques to create your very own country finishes.

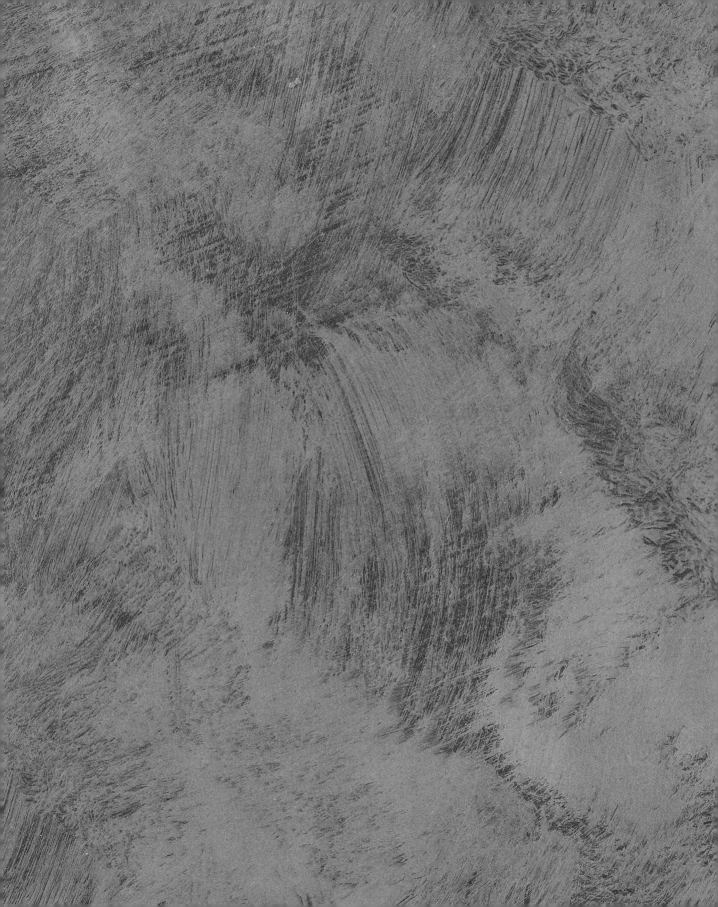

BASIC TECHNIQUES

Searching for and finding furniture and accessories to refinish can be a lot of fun. In fact, I have always found the hunt to be one of the most enjoyable parts of the whole process. Once you begin looking, you'll discover things from a surprising number of unexpected sources.

Make some time to carefully investigate your attic, garage, and basement; then try to arrange to visit the attics of relatives. Finding a neglected or forgotten piece with some family history is a real coup, and the pleasure of returning it to use in your environment is immeasurable.

Check the yellow pages under "Furniture — Used" for local retailers that handle potential cast-off treasures. Goodwill Industries and the Salvation Army have retail stores with furniture departments in many towns and cities. Church rummage sales are another good source for furnishings. Be on the lookout for tag sales, garage sales, and yard sales. You'll often find them listed in the classified section of the newspaper on Friday and Saturday.

This is a good time to acquaint yourself with the major regional antique fairs, sources of a tremendous selection of quality furniture. To learn where the big antique fairs are in your region, look in reader service magazines like *Country Living, House Beautiful, Decorating and Remodeling,* and *Metropolitan Home.* They often publish information on antique fairs in their late spring issues. Ask for information in antique shops, and watch your local paper for listings of these shows. While you're at it, check out the classified section for estate sales. Try to get there early; the best stuff usually goes pretty quickly. Often, the best source of information is the grapevine. Check with friends and keep your ear to the ground. You might be pleasantly surprised by what turns up.

Call a friend and suggest browsing through the neighborhood antique shops. Make a day of it. Have some lunch, then really explore all those dark nooks and crannies. Dress comfortably and be prepared to get a little dirty. It's more than worth it for the special thrill of finding that unique object, perfect for your home.

I continue to find interesting things in shops that I visit frequently. One favorite shop of mine in North Carolina has a back room that's more like a warehouse, with endless sets of furniture, mantels, columns, and other architectural elements and fragments. It always holds new surprises. Visit your resources regularly, because new things come in all the time. Try to find out which days new items are delivered so you can get first crack at them.

Most cities have at least a couple of stores that sell unfinished pine and other wood furniture. Mastercraft is a manufacturer that offers a broad range of unfinished furniture for the home; it can be found in stores like Naked Furniture and other chain stores that handle relatively inexpensive new pieces.

Traditional wicker furniture comes in a variety of styles — some of it very lacy, delicate, and weblike. Other pieces are much more solid in form, even contemporary in their design. They're available from a number of sources throughout the United States: specialty stores, high-end retail shops, and some very well designed and effectively packaged chain stores like Pier 1 Imports, Wicker World, and Conran's. A number of style-setting catalogs such as Crate & Barrel, Pottery Barn, and Smith & Hawken offer updated variations of traditional wicker forms, as do major stores like Sears and JCPenney.

As you can see, there's no shortage of resources for new and used furnishings appropriate for refinishing and painting. Take your time, and remember the goal is to have fun throughout this process.

DESIGN CONSIDERATIONS

Where does one come up with colors? The color you choose to paint a piece may simply be your favorite. Sometimes color choices are inspired by other furniture in the room, as well as by things like wall and floor coverings or fabrics.

You can find color ideas almost anywhere. You pass by many things and unconsciously process a lot of visual information in the course of a day. Sources of inspiration are everywhere, from magazines to the natural environment.

Make note of pleasing color relationships and contrasts when you discover them. When you're in the supermarket, for example, pause for a moment and look at that stack of lemons. Notice the texture as well as the color. Look at what's next to and around them — oranges, limes, grapes, plums. Consider the combinations that are most interesting to you.

Keep in mind, however, that while lemon yellow and cobalt blue make a stunning color combination, a piece of furniture painted those colors might seem like a siren or blinking light in your home, demanding attention and overpowering the other furnishings in the room. You can turn down the volume on the colors that inspired you, using shades like ochre and midnight blue for a more subtle and pleasing result.

Learn to recognize potential in a piece you wouldn't previously have given a second glance. Begin to look at things in a creative way. Whether you're cleaning out the attic or perusing the Salvation Army store, look at the lines of the piece and imagine it covered over with color. Evaluate its scale, note any special detailing. Look for good construction and joints. Be careful not to paint real antiques, however, because you may significantly reduce their value.

There are many possibilities and variations with each piece of furniture you paint. One of the pleasures of all of this is making the decisions about your color palette and figuring out what you want the finished piece to be like. You begin to make these decisions by sketching, coloring with markers or pencils, or by going to the hardware store and selecting paint samples.

Not only should you heighten your awareness of color combinations, textures, and patterns; you should also begin to consider the

element of light. You may be a bright-light person or a candlelight person. Just how does light affect your furnishings, and how will light in your rooms play against your choice of colors? Bring some paint color samples home from the hardware store and test them by laying them on a piece of your upholstered furniture, or taping them on a wall and living with them for a few days. See how the colors change throughout the day as the light in the room changes. The intensity of light will have a direct effect on the way the colors you choose interact with the rest of your room.

Remember, you're striving for a visual harmony in your environment, a harmony that reflects a careful blending of texture and color value. There's nothing wrong with a bold piece that stands out and calls some attention to itself, but it shouldn't be so dominating that it can't coexist with the other objects in your room: the wall covering, the upholstery, and whatever other elements are a part of the environment.

TOOLS AND MATERIALS

You won't need any unusual or expensive supplies for the projects in this book. Almost all the products you'll be using are nontoxic and water soluble, including strippers and polyurethane. No special solvents are necessary; soap and water are all you'll need for cleaning up.

You probably already have much of what you need around the house. If not, you can easily purchase supplies from a general hardware store or home improvement center. In addition to the materials listed for individual projects in this book, it's a good idea to keep certain things handy at all times. Some of these are indispensable, such as drop cloths, scrub sponges, kitchen sponges, rags, a plastic bucket, steel wool, sandpaper, and tack cloth. These are all essential for general cleaning of your piece and for lightly roughing up the surface in preparation for paint, stain, or a protective coating.

I can't say enough about the sponge. Almost every project will require at least one type of sponge in some way, so you'll want to keep your sponges always within reach. After your hand, they're the most important tool you'll use.

The kitchen sponge is indispensable as a scrubber and wiper. I use those yellow-and-green combination sponges from the supermarket. The green (pot scrubber) side is great for scrubbing off an overcolor; and then I just turn it over to the yellow (cellulose) side to lift and remove loosened pigment.

The scrub pad is another useful tool for removing paint or roughing up a surface. The Scotch brand from 3M is widely available. It can be used in the stripping process as well as for removing overcolor. These pads come in two grades of coarseness; one is similar to the scrubber side of a combination kitchen sponge, the other is much more abrasive.

Sea sponges — the kind you find in bath shops or the paint section of hardware stores — apply paint to a surface with an interesting, natural texture, and are used in some of the projects here for sponging on overcolor.

You can use newspaper, an old bedsheet, perhaps a canvas tarpaulin if you have one, to protect your work surface and your floor from paint splatters. I prefer the convenience of inexpensive paper drop cloths. They have both an absorbent paper side and a moisture-repellent plastic side. They're easy to fold up and store, and can be reused for many projects. It's also not a bad idea to have some Scott Rags-in-a-Box on hand. I find they last longer than paper towels and are durable as well as absorbent.

You'll need a stripping product, a scraper or putty knife, and a few other things to help you remove an old finish. Materials and details on stripping are covered later in this chapter.

Sandpaper and steel wool are available in a variety of grades. No matter which one you're using, begin the process with a medium grade and finish up with finer grade. On raw wood, these abrasives clean up rough edges and smooth the surface for whatever application is to follow. You'll also use them to rough up a painted surface on which you plan to apply another coat of paint.

Tack cloth is basically just cheesecloth treated with a waxy, tacky substance that dust, lint, sawdust, and steel wool fibers cling to. Wipe your furniture pieces down with tack cloth as the final step before applying paint or stain. Use tack cloth if you're sanding between coats as well.

Set yourself up with a small variety of paintbrushes. You don't have to spend a lot of money to do this. For applying paint or varnish stripper, use a good-quality natural or nylon bristle brush. For painting large surfaces relatively quickly, I like those inexpensive foam (or sponge) brushes. They're easy to handle, hold a good amount of paint without dripping or splattering, and provide a great deal of control during application. They're available in various widths and can be washed out and reused many times. For fine lines and detail work, you'll need a couple of artist's brushes, as well as a short-bristled stencil brush for stenciling and scumbling. Ask for help in the art supply store if you're unsure what to purchase. Most clerks in art supply stores are artists themselves and should certainly be able to handle the majority of questions you'd come up with. It's not a bad idea to get acquainted with one particular employee whom you can call on regularly.

Latex and acrylic paints are probably the single biggest shortcut to an attractive country finish, and are what makes it possible to complete most of these projects within a few hours or a weekend. The soap-and-water cleanup is an obvious advantage, and they speed drying time tremendously over oil-based products. If you were using oil-based paint, not only would you need excellent ventilation and a solvent like kerosene or mineral spirits for cleanup, you'd have to wait twenty-four hours between coats.

When you're covering large surface areas (like the barn-red base coat on the dresser pictured on page 54) use quart containers of premixed or custom-mixed latex eggshell-finish paint. It will be easier to work with and certainly more economical than small tubes of acrylic paint. The tube paints can be used for details, accents, and overcolors, to name a few. Visit an art supply store and explore the racks of premixed acrylic artist colors. They come in shades that reflect the colors of nature: berries, wheat, grasses, sky, and the like. You can mix these colors further, adding black to a forest green, for example, for an even deeper shade. When custom-mixing colors for any project, it is a very good idea to write down your color "recipe," because invariably you will run out of paint and need to mix up more.

Some projects require the use of masking tape or painter's tape for sharp, clean edges. Masking tape is available from many sources in a variety of widths, and painter's tape can be found wherever house paint is sold. There's more specific information on using these products in the section on masking, page 33.

Some of the projects in this book involve the application of stenciled designs. If your tastes and interests lead you toward simple, geometric patterns like the checkerboard, there's no rea-son to painstakingly cut the stencil by hand. I recommend a look through the precut stencils available in art supply stores and craft stores; even some nurseries have a section with art or craft items. You'll find many sizes and variations on the checkerboard, as well as other simple, country-inspired designs. Hopefully, the section on stenciling will inspire you to create some of your own original stencil patterns. For this you'll need some stencil paper — a white, glossy, medium-weight paper that can be either opaque or translucent. For cutting original or custom stencils, I prefer the translucent paper, which enables you to more easily see the line you're cutting. To do the cutting, you'll need a stencil knife or matt knife. You can also use an X-acto knife, utility knife, or any razor knife you can comfortably handle, provided it has a sharp blade.

Consult the resource section at the back of this book for specific product names and manufacturers' addresses. All the products listed are nationally distributed, so don't be shy about asking someone at your hardware store to help you find them.

In addition to all the items mentioned here, I personally find a good supply of apples and KitKats or M&M's to be indispensable.

SETTING UP YOUR WORK SPACE

Choose a place to work that has a good supply of light available. If you can work outside, that's terrific. If you're working indoors, inexpensive clip-on lamps are helpful, because they can quickly be adjusted to eliminate shadows and keep your piece in the best possible light.

It's preferable to work near a convenient source of water, such as an outdoor spigot, the

kitchen sink, or a basement slop sink. If these aren't options for you, keep a bucket or two of fresh water nearby. Place them out of your way but within reach. Accidentally stepping into or knocking over a bucket of murky paint water will take some of the enjoyment out of working on your project.

You'll also need a work surface that's a comfortable height for you, to use as a place for laying out your materials as well as for working on smaller furniture pieces and accessories. You can raise your kitchen table a little by using bricks, books, or whatever it takes to elevate the surface so you're able to work on your project without feeling physical strain.

Before you start any project that involves paint, protect the areas around your work. Again, if you're fortunate enough to be able to work outside, simply put a drop cloth on the ground. If you're working inside on a table, however, cover the table and also place another drop cloth on the floor under you. Keep rags close by in case of mishaps.

You'll be working with things like water-based latex acrylic paint, Woodfinisher's Pride, and Varethane water-based polyurethane, none of which contains any poisonous fumes. Good ventilation is preferable, nonetheless, because it helps pieces dry more quickly.

So with a comfortable, protected work surface, water, adequate light, and good ventilation, you're ready to begin.

PREPARING THE SURFACE

The first step for virtually all country finish treatments is to prepare the surface. What does that mean? For some treatments, it may only mean washing the piece down with a soap-and-water solution and drying it thoroughly. For other treatments, surface preparation will involve stripping, sanding, then rubbing down with tack cloth to remove any loose sawdust particles clinging to the wood. A new, unfinished piece will probably require only a light once-over with some steel wool and a tack cloth.

In a nutshell, preparing the surface means removing any protective coatings, wax, oil, and dirt to make the surface receptive to a new coat of paint or stain. After a thorough cleaning, small blemishes — dents, gouges, nail holes — can be filled with wood putty and lightly sanded smooth.

One important point about water: When washing down a piece of furniture, do it quickly and dry it off promptly with clean rags or paper towels. Then let it air dry for an hour or so. If you let water sit on wood for more than a few minutes, it begins to raise the grain and damage the surface. Also, once the wood becomes moist, it must dry out thoroughly before you apply paint, stain, or sealer.

If you plan to pickle or stain (that is, use translucent pigments that leave the wood grain visible) you'll need to remove old paint and take the piece down to its bare bones. If you intend to paint the piece, however, it may be a waste of your time to strip it down to raw wood. You can always go that extra step, but the truth is, you really only need to rough up the existing painted surface enough to give the new coat of paint a good base to adhere to. That's where your sandpaper and steel wool come in handy. If carved details on your piece are becoming too subtle or are getting lost completely under multiple coats of paint, you'll probably want to strip that paint away regardless, to restore the clarity of those details.

If you're refinishing old or new wicker, you must prepare the surface by removing any sealant or protective coating so the wicker fibers can absorb the paint, stain, or other treatment you plan to apply. This is a good outdoor project for a sunny day, but it could be done just as easily in your kitchen if you lay down some protective pads or newspaper and use a nonpoisonous stripping gel like Woodfinisher's Pride varnish remover, a biodegradable, water-soluble, and nonflammable product. Following label directions, simply apply the gel with a brush, then wash it off with rubbing alcohol. Afterward, the whole surface should be washed clean, wiped down, and thoroughly dried. Allow the piece to dry for a good twenty-four hours so moisture locked within the fibers of the furniture will evaporate. Use your vacuum attachment to remove any debris from the weave.

Remember, it's not necessary to overprepare your furniture or accessories. How you prepare the surface will largely be dictated by your own common sense and your vision of what the finished piece will be.

STRIPPING

Stripping away old paint and varnish will be necessary to provide the best base possible on which to apply some of your country finishes. The process of stripping and refinishing furniture used to be unpleasant and hazardous, because all the products that did the job were highly toxic and flammable. They couldn't be safely used in your home, so you were pretty much restricted to the yard, garage, or basement. In the basement, you had to turn off your hot water heater because of the flammable nature of the product, adding the inconvenience of no heat or hot water.

Fortunately, all of this has changed with the recent availability of some new, safe stripping products. They're nonpoisonous, water soluble, and biodegradable, and they do a great job. With our growing concern for the environment, it's only logical to avoid hazardous materials if at all possible, instead choosing products that won't harm us. The advent of these safe strippers enables you to strip and refinish indoors, allowing even an apartment dweller the satisfaction and pride that come from successfully refinishing a piece of furniture. Stripping can now be done with such ease it makes refinishing a pleasure, allowing you to focus on the fun of watching a piece be transformed rather than the former drudgery of the process itself.

I use a stripping product called Woodfinisher's Pride. It comes in two formulations, a paint-stripping gel and a varnish-stripping gel. They remove oil-based paint, enamel, and latex paint, as well as varnish, shellac, polyurethane, and lacquer. Because Woodfinisher's Pride is formulated as a gel, it clings to vertical and horizontal surfaces without running, and you can coat an entire project in one step. Its Breathe-Easy formula can be used indoors with proper ventilation, and the method of application and removal is the same whether you're using the paint remover or the varnish remover.

Choose a place to work that has good ventilation and lighting, and make sure you have all the needed materials on hand before you begin. Some good music might make the job more fun.

MATERIALS

drop cloth

stripping gel

paintbrush

scraper or putty knife

steel wool

rag or paper toweling

scrub sponge

rubbing alcohol

wood filler

sandpaper

tack cloth

1. Arrange a drop cloth or other material to protect your work area. Open stripping gel and, following the manufacturer's recommendations and instructions, begin to brush a thick coat — 1/8 to 1/4 inch — onto the piece of furniture. While you can coat the entire piece at once, you may prefer to work in sections, to avoid becoming frustrated if the process turns out to be taking too long. Allow the gel to work for 30 minutes or so, and test a small section to see if the finish is ready to be removed. The surface should have bubbled up somewhat by this time, indicating it's ready.

2. Remove the gel and paint or varnish residue with your scraper or putty knife. Use a gentle but deliberate pulling or plowing motion, taking care not to gouge the wood. Plowing means pushing the scraper away from you along the wood grain, collecting the stripping gel on the top of the scraper. Pulling the scraper toward you along the wood surface will cause the scraped gel to collect on the bottom. Either method works well; it's really a matter of personal preference. Again, try to work with the grain of the wood so you don't accidentally scar the surface.

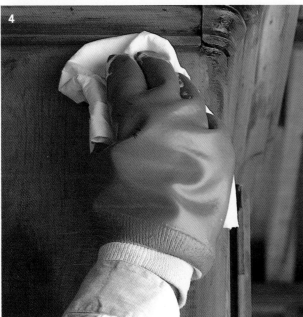

3. Use a medium-grade steel wool to remove the gel and paint residue from rounded or carved surfaces. Once you've scraped off all the gel, wipe down with a rag or some paper toweling, then use steel wool or a scrub sponge and some rubbing alcohol to finish cleaning the surface of the piece. This will loosen any remaining pigment and residue left by the stripping gel. Continue washing off the surface with the alcohol and rub down with a clean sponge until the surface is clean. Since Woodfinisher's Pride is water soluble, you can wash out your sponges and scraper with a mild soap-and-water solution.

4. Certain areas of the piece may require a second application of stripper — inset or carved designs, for example. The key here is to wait those thirty minutes and let the gel do the work for you. Once the piece is clean and dry, finish the job by rubbing down with a medium steel wool, working your way down through the finer grades. This will clean out the pores of the wood and get the surface completely ready for a new pigment or finish. Any surface blemishes can be filled with wood filler and lightly sanded until smooth. Use tack cloth to remove any sawdust or steel wool fibers. At this point, the piece is ready to stain or paint.

PAINTING AND SCRUBBING

Many processes in this book mimic historic European and Early American finishes whose surfaces, through generations of use, have worn away layers and established marvelous textures and patinas. You will apply one coat of paint, then another in a different color, then scrub, sand, or sponge some of it away. By doing these processes you will be engaging in building specific steps that will enable you to better understand the techniques behind all painted finishes.

Before painting, make sure the piece is fully dry and that it has been wiped clean of any surface debris with tack cloth. Have everything you'll need nearby — paint, brushes, rags, water, and the like. Paint surfaces evenly, following the grain. Be modest with your application; don't slop the paint on and allow it to drip. Your goal is an even coat that covers the surface in an opaque way.

You can use old cups and dishes as your palette. I prefer shallow bowls because you can thoroughly mix new colors in them and they can easily be covered with plastic wrap to prevent the paint from drying out between coats. Deli containers — the kind you get when you purchase premade salads — are great for mixing and storing paint because of their tight-fitting lids. Incidentally, if you're going to have to come back to a particular color, you can also prevent your wet brushes from drying out by covering them with a piece of plastic wrap for a few hours or even overnight. This saves you the time of washing your brushes out right away, then again after a second coat.

No matter what you're using to apply a texture or painted design, blot, wipe, or test it first to avoid paint blobs. If you're using a brush, wipe it on the rim of the can before painting the intended surface. If you're using a sponge to apply an overcolor, blot the sponge first on the palette or some newspaper. You can always apply the paint more heavily if you've underdone it. Overdoing it, however, may mean you have to start again from scratch.

Economy of effort — getting the job done without wasting steps — is something to consider. Try not to keep circling the piece when you're painting. With your feet comfortably planted, paint everything you can see and conveniently reach before moving yourself, the piece, or the paint. Be methodical. This minimizes the likelihood of mishaps, such as dumping your paint or stepping on the cat.

When painting something with rungs or other details, like a chair or a wicker piece, I usually start with the piece upside down to ensure complete coverage. Don't paint the bottom of chair legs or table legs, however. Once the piece is in use, that paint would very likely come off onto the floor or carpet. If you like, cover the bottom tips of chair and table legs with a small piece of masking tape before you begin.

Many older pieces you'll find at flea markets or tag sales are already painted, which presents some interesting design choices. I like the idea of not always starting a country finish technique with a freshly painted piece. You can apply fresh paint as a first step, but if you have a piece that's already painted a beautiful color, consider that a base on which to build. If the piece has some flawed or highly damaged areas, you can blend those areas to make them more unified, more complete, and more wholly acceptable for your living space without losing that great color. In this way, you are enriching the existing character of the piece as opposed to fabricating a new one.

If you're preparing a piece that's already painted, remember that you can choose to remove only some of the pigment, allowing some of it to remain as your base, which you can then highlight and enhance.

The instructions for most of the projects in this book call for two coats of base color. This provides a superior foundation for whatever treatment is to follow. If one coat seems to have covered the piece adequately, however, you could choose to move on to the next step, particularly if you're painting a second coat of another color, then sealing with wax or polyurethane.

In general, when removing overcolor (the top coat), you are deliberately exposing the undercolor (or undercoat) to bring to the piece a convincing illusion of wear created by repeated handling over many years. Think about where the piece would have had the most handling. Look at corners and drawer pulls. Open and close doors to see where your hands touch them. When you reach for a door pull, where do your nails come in contact with the piece? With a chair, the arms, seat, and seat back should show signs of use. Remember, making the surface less uniform is the key to the whole concept of the country finish. Surface variations convey a sense of age and use, and can really give newly painted furniture a timeworn feeling. The amazing thing is that it takes only a few minutes to transform a piece into something that looks and feels a hundred years old.

Keep in mind that if the overcolor you've chosen is a lighter shade than the undercolor — beige over deep green, for example — it will probably require two coats for complete coverage. Allow the first coat to dry, sand lightly, then wipe down with tack cloth and apply the second coat.

When removing overcolor, be careful about how much water you use. If you put too much water on your sponge and the paint itself absorbs that water, you're likely to wipe away all of your paint. There's a delicate balance of touch and correct degree of moisture that will determine how much or how little paint you remove. Even a small amount of experience will teach you how much or how little pressure you should apply. All of these things will become second nature to you once you have experimented with them and once you've done a couple of pieces. Remember, you can easily repeat the process of painting and removing on areas where you may have fumbled.

What you're creating is a surface that makes the piece appear aged and worn. The success of this process and a pleasing end result depends upon your touch. A hard, heavy hand will take off too much paint; too light a hand will not remove enough. Strive for a balance and consistency so that your new finish will have a timeworn yet natural-looking patina. If you wish to expose more of the undercolor, simply repeat the scrubbing process and rewipe. If you're a little unsure of yourself, do it in small stages. Stand back and look at the piece from time to time. This allows you a great deal of control over the process, and you're likely to be much happier with the results. It will also eliminate the need to repaint areas you may have scrubbed too hard or too long. If you find you've overdone it, repaint and allow the piece to dry, then with a lighter hand begin the removal process again.

While scrubbing, you'll be exerting pressure and creating a rhythm, an internal rhythm that is transferred or applied to the piece you're working on through the motions and gestures of your arm and hand. This part of the process is, for me, a contemplative time, one not dissimilar to rowing, ironing, or gardening, and it produces a certain satisfaction and understanding of the whole experience. It's a very personal and individual component of the refinishing process, and is something you'll be using and relying on when exploring other country finish techniques.

Keep in mind the fact that you can't really ruin a piece with paint. It's very simple and only a little time-consuming to wipe it down or let it dry and start over. If you're unhappy with your country finish, simply erase it and begin again when you have the time and the right frame of mind. The only thing you've lost is a little time, but you've also gained some new insights that you'll apply in future furniture-painting endeavors. Don't compromise, because you will never be satisfied with the piece. You want to be able to say, if only to yourself, "I did this, and I'm proud of it."

You should begin any painting process — sponging, splattering — by testing a small area first, experimenting with different color combinations, either on the piece itself or a scrap piece of wood or paper. Maintain a light but deliberate hand, and you'll have the feel of it in no time. When you have that feel for it, go right to your piece with confidence. Don't be afraid to make mistakes. They'll teach you more than your successes.

It's important to keep standing back and evaluating your work. Be in touch with where the piece and the process are going. Don't hesitate to have fun with a country finish, but be careful not to overdo it.

There's a very fine line between a painted piece that's whimsical and spirited and one that's overdone or tacky. Of course, this is a matter determined by personal taste. The point is that although you can continue adding interesting details to a painted piece, it's important you know when to stop.

MASKING

Masking tape is used in a variety of ways throughout this book. It's helpful when creating lines and borders, and in blocking off certain sections of furniture for paint treatments. Different effects can be achieved by using tape of different widths. You can take shortcuts with masking tape as well, using the width of the tape as a measuring tool. The placement of the borderline on top of Arthur's bench (page 105), for example, was determined by using short pieces of masking tape to establish a uniform interval between the long strips of tape that defined the border. This eliminated the need for a ruler or the additional steps of marking and erasing pencil lines.

Unlike many of the other, more organic sorts of processes in this book, masking gives you well-defined bands of separation or segregation of color and texture, and is most appropriate for creating designs of a symmetrical or geometric character.

Masking tape is available in a variety of widths and tackinesses, and is very easy to find in hardware, craft, or art supply stores. Painting tape (or painter's tape) is used primarily by housepainters, but it has advantages over mask-

ing tape for certain country-finish applications. It's wider than most masking tape — two inches — and one-third of the surface area of the tape has no tack, or adhesive, making it easy to move, reposition, and reuse. Sometimes regular masking tape will pull up recently dried paint, but painting tape is very gentle on painted surfaces. It adheres well and provides a crisp, clean line.

When using any masking tape, it's very important to rub the paint edge of the tape firmly on the surface so paint won't seep under it. If you peel up the tape and find that paint has pooled under the edge, it might set you back to zero. Remove masking tape within twenty-four hours — three hours if it has been exposed to sunlight. Remember, masking tape can pull up a freshly painted surface, so you want to be sure the base you're starting with is completely dry.

FINISHING TOUCHES

When latex paint dries, it forms a durable finish that doesn't usually require additional sealing or protection, which is why it is used to paint walls and woodwork around the house. For furniture and accessories, however, you'll be using latex paint in a more creative way to produce finishes with subtle details and variations. Because these pieces will be subjected to use, you must add a final protective coating to seal and protect the piece. This also enhances the surface, enriches the colors, and helps the piece hold its finished appearance longer. You have a few options at this stage.

For many projects in this book, I've used Butcher's wax, a clear or amber-tinted paste wax that's also used on bowling alleys. In most instances, I prefer to use clear Butcher's wax, but the amber variety adds a subtle golden tint that helps create an illusion of age. Simply follow the directions on the can; apply the wax, let it dry for twenty minutes or so, and buff the surface with a clean rag or an electric polisher. It brings out all of the richness of the pigment itself, and subtle details become clearer to the eye. Butcher's wax can be reapplied, and it creates a surface finish that works well, neither glossy nor matte, just a good sheen that protects the piece and adds a nice final touch.

Varethane water-based polyurethane is available in high-gloss as well as medium-luster and low-luster finish options. Which one you choose is really determined by your taste and personal preference, but I don't suggest a high-gloss polyurethane for most pieces. It calls attention to itself and can reflect light in a way that highlights every character flaw and surface imperfection. Polyurethane is a more durable and practical surface finish than Butcher's wax for pieces you intend to use in a casual environment, or pieces that have to stand up to high use, food and liquids, and children. It can be washed or wiped down with a damp cloth.

Polyurethane is applied with a paintbrush. One coat may suffice, but two or more coats will give you a very durable finish. For best results, wipe the surface down with a fine-grade steel wool then with tack cloth between coats.

Now that you're familiar with the basic techniques, you're ready to begin the hunt. Search with confidence and a level head, and look for the furnishings you'd like to give a country finish. This is one of the most enjoyable parts of the whole process. Have fun with it.

Analyze your home and consider where to place a newly refinished and painted piece of furniture. It's easy to become overly enthusiastic, so be sure your labor is well spent. Carefully plot out each project before you begin, completely thinking through each process first. Gather color samples and, if necessary, mix a few colors and try them out. Take your time. Your efforts will pay off handsomely.

Don't clutter up your home with a vast number of unrelated painted finishes, however. Your newly finished piece should be in the right space and reflect the correct palette for your room. The "less is more" theory really applies here. Choose pieces and determine their placements carefully to establish or maintain the balance and harmony between what you've created and the existing furnishings in your home.

All the techniques and projects in this book are designed for you to master and accomplish within a few hours. Inside of a couple of weekends, you can create enough pieces to redecorate your home.

As you read through the rest of the book, refer back to this chapter for tips on the basic techniques. For detailed explanations of specific processes, such as sponging or stenciling, consult the index. The instructions that accompany the projects are written in a way that should enable you to closely reproduce them. I don't expect you to re-create the projects exactly, but rather to use them and the detailed explanations as a starting point. Look at how I've done something, then figure out how to apply the principles to your own piece, making your own color and design choices. This book and the projects in it should inspire your own creativity. Take the process used on Arthur's bench (page 105) and apply it to a table, or transfer the technique used on the plaid box (page 92) to your dresser. Use this book as your resource and guide; experiment with as many or as few techniques as you wish, and remember that you have the ability to produce many creative variations.

It's important to remember to seek out only nonhazardous products. All the materials you need to safely transform your furniture are available from a variety of sources. Check the materials section at the end of the book for more information on these products. You'll feel good about protecting yourself as well as our earth.

PAINT-AND-SCRUB TECHNIQUES

For most paint-over-stain projects, you must begin by removing any wax or other protective sealer from the furniture so it's receptive to the paint. You'll paint the piece, using the stained surface as the undercolor. If you're starting with a light-colored unpainted piece, you can give it a softer, darker patina by staining it before painting. When you remove some of the paint, or overcolor, the stain will be revealed, creating a surface with a subtle richness, depth, and texture. Many projects in this book involve the manipulation of an overcolor and undercolor, so you'll see those terms a lot. The interplay of two or more layers of color on a surface can make a piece appear worn and aged.

The simple paint-and-scrub technique used on the wicker set is one of the most basic of all the techniques we're going to explore in *Country Finishes.* As you become more confident and more creative, you should explore further, experimenting with additional colors and techniques. If your wicker piece has a complex woven pattern or detail on a seat back, you might highlight it with a color that picks up the fabric or another element in the room. One of the real satisfactions of creating your own surface treatments is the ability to personalize and customize your piece to fit a room setting.

WICKER SET Wicker furniture is very popular and has been for centuries. There is a sense of romance about wicker pieces, fixtures on the grand porches of classic old summer homes, silent sentinels framing panoramic views. Wicker stretched along oceanfronts for generations, but it was also found in Victorian city homes, garden gazebos, and the plains of the Midwest. Wicker has always been at home in casual environments, and for a long time, that's where it stayed. Recently, however, it has come inside, where it blends beautifully with wood and upholstered furnishings.

I found this stained wicker set in a North Carolina shop that I visit frequently. The fabric for the cushions was chosen to complement the space the wicker was intended for, with color cues taken from the putty trim and cranberry shutters. The putty-color paint used on the furniture provides a neutral base that also reflects the stone walls of the house.

This paint-and-scrub treatment shows the original wicker surface and the newly applied paint in a way that makes the furniture appear pretty timeworn. The completed set makes the porch a very inviting and comfortable place to enjoy coffee and the morning paper.

MATERIALS
interior latex paint: putty color, eggshell finish
2-inch paintbrush
combination kitchen sponge
water-based polyurethane
polyurethane brush

1. Starting with clean, dry stained wicker, paint the entire surface putty color, using a 2-inch brush. Start with the piece upside down to make sure you get into all the cracks and crevices. After you've painted one full side, turn the piece, tipping and propping it up, and continue to cover the other three sides. It should take about an hour for the paint to dry.

2. Using the abrasive side of a moistened combination kitchen sponge, scrub gently over the painted surface with short rotary motions, following the flow of the weave, to remove some of the paint and reveal the stained surface. Lift and remove the loosened paint with the cellulose side of the sponge. Rinse the sponge in water frequently.

3. Allow wicker to dry completely — about 24 hours — and apply a sealing finish coat of water-based satin polyurethane.

BOW BENCH I used to have two bow benches on my porch, and their lines lent a soft grace to the entrance of my home for a number of seasons. I bought this Windsor bow bench because it had good, clean lines and a gently arched back, which I liked. It seemed to me this was a versatile piece that could be useful in several environments, whether as end seating for dining, as a comfortable entrance seat in the foyer, or at the foot of a bed.

The bench had a surface coating of wax over its golden oak stain. I began this country finish treatment by removing the wax, which required scrubbing with steel wool, then washing down with Murphy's Oil Soap. My goal in treating the bench was to provide you with a few tricks and techniques to help you create an appearance of age.

Your creative decisions will determine the spirit, character, and final appearance of the surface. These decisions should be influenced by where and how you intend to use the piece. Perhaps you plan to add pillows or a seat cushion. These are reflections of your artistic voice and design sensibilities.

This project is a delightful weekend's worth of work that will yield a beautiful addition to your home. Remember that with each of these projects, you can apply the illustrated techniques to almost any surface. However, though it is a lot of fun, you should resist the temptation to flyspeck your whole house.

MATERIALS

steel wool

Murphy's Oil Soap

acrylic paint: barn red, black, ochre

paintbrush

extra-fine sandpaper

tack cloth

scrub pad

sponge or rag

small, soft-bristled watercolor brush

toothbrush

spray bottle

Butcher's wax

1. Prepare surface with steel wool and Murphy's Oil Soap, as described above, then paint entire bench with deep barn-red acrylic and allow to dry. Sand the surface lightly, wipe with tack cloth, paint second coat, and allow to dry.

2. Use a moistened scrub pad to gently scrub off some of the paint and expose the stain. Remove more paint from areas that would logically have sustained the most wear over time: the arms, parts of the seat, the legs and struts. Use long gestures and a light touch during this process. Short scrubbing motions won't yield "authentic" results. Remember to wipe off the loosened paint with a damp sponge or rag.

3. Accent the grooves on the legs and struts using a small, soft-bristled watercolor brush and black acrylic paint.

4. Next, dip an old toothbrush into the black paint and drag your thumb across the bristles to lightly spatter the paint onto the surface, adding "flyspecks," first around the grooves, then over the entire surface of the bench. Practice this technique beforehand on paper to learn how to control the spattering paint. Slight variations in thumb pressure and the angle at which you hold the toothbrush will determine the pattern.

5. Put some diluted acrylic ochre paint (about half water and half paint) in a spray bottle — an old cleaning-product bottle with a trigger pump will do nicely — and randomly spray the surface of the bench. These spots will be larger than the flyspecks, adding a character, depth, and texture to the piece that makes the finish far more interesting.

6. Once the black and ochre specks have dried, go over the surface again with your sponge to remove some of them. Blend and erase certain areas so the bench doesn't appear to have a sprayed and fabricated surface. Surface variations make a piece appear more authentic than consistent, all-over patterns. The goal is to create a surface that looks as though it has evolved over time, showing signs of wear and use. Finish with an application of amber Butcher's wax and buff to a low luster.

KITCHEN CHAIRS
Here's an easy project I like a lot. It involves minimal addition of paint, yet quickly dresses up ordinary chairs with an original pattern and makes a strong country finish statement.

These old kitchen chairs were purchased with a light stain and were to be used with a country kitchen table I've had for a while. They illustrate how a color treatment on a small area of a piece of furniture can have a dramatic impact. This project took very little time and is a perfect example of a treatment you can complete in a few hours over a weekend. The longest and most tedious part of the job is the prep work, then waiting for the chair to be completely dry before resealing it.

The design goal was to coordinate the chairs to the table, which was done by bringing an element of one to the other. I took a color cue from the green table base and legs and translated it onto the chair in a very straightforward way that considers the architecture of the chair. I also used a sponge and some black paint to create what looks like folk graining. It doesn't mimic or reflect the grain of any specific wood but is a decorative texture with a certain spontaneity and energy about it. I wanted the chair backs to be random and mismatched, with a design that felt immediate and spirited.

Incidentally, that masked and painted area on the seat back would serve as a good base for a number of painted accents; it could have been combed, stippled, stenciled, or simply outlined. The possibilities are infinite and the creative choices are yours. The same treatment applied on the chair back could very easily have been translated to the seat as well, simply by following the contour of the seat with masking tape to define the area for painting.

This is a simple, clean, and direct color application that alters the character yet maintains the integrity of the chair. It successfully unifies the chairs and the table, turning them into a set.

MATERIALS
steel wool
1/2-inch masking tape
acrylic paint: green, black
paintbrushes
sea sponge
Butcher's wax

1. Remove protective surface coating of areas to be painted by rubbing chair down lightly with steel wool. Wash entire chair with soap and water, wipe down thoroughly, and allow to dry. Following the line of the outer edge of the seat back, apply a border of 1/2-inch masking tape, creating an inner rectangle or field on which to apply the paint. Mask around the back support rungs above and below grooved lines. Paint the inner rectangle and the back support accent with premixed green acrylic paint and allow to dry.

2. Place a small amount of black acrylic paint on a palette, and dip edge of sea sponge into paint. Blot or dab sponge on dry area of palette (this reduces the chance of accidentally applying blobs of paint to the surface). Sweep sponge across green surface in soft arcing motions, first in one direction, then the other.

3, 4. Randomly dab the sponge on the outer back supports and taped accents. Wipe surfaces with opposite side of sponge (or a clean rag or paper towel) to soften lines and create burls. Remove masking tape. When paint is completely dry, seal with clear Butcher's wax. Allow to dry for 20 minutes, then buff to a satin luster with a clean dry cloth or electric polisher.

The techniques used to create a paint-over-paint country finish are very similar to those explored with the paint-over-stain finishes. It's basically about removing part of the top coat, or overcolor, to expose some of the undercoat, or undercolor. In this case, what is revealed by scrubbing the surface is not a tinted wood grain but an opaque layer of paint. This technique opens up wider possibilities for bolder color contrasts and combinations. Your creative challenges include selecting the piece of furniture itself, the room in which you intend to use it, and colors that complement one another.

You can use new unfinished (or naked) furniture or an already painted piece you'd rather not have to strip. Let's assume you have a harvest gold dining room table, and you want to change the color or character of the table without first returning it to its natural wood surface. You can just paint over it with the new dominant colors, using the gold as your base, or undercolor. The original gold surface then becomes the foundation of your country finish treatment.

Many different looks can be created using paint-over-paint techniques. Furnishings and accessories can be covered in an opaque or translucent way and allowed to dry, then be manipulated and textured with a sponged-on application of additional complementary colors; you can "comb" through a layer of wet paint to create a primitive-looking folk-grain finish; you can splatter a piece using a toothbrush dipped in paint to create an interesting texture and depth. Many variations are possible within these techniques, depending mainly on your taste and your touch with a brush, scrub sponge, or steel wool. The possibilities are unlimited, and the results can be very soft and subtle or rich and dramatic.

DRESSER One of the real challenges in creating a country finish is working with a new, unfinished piece. These naked forms appear so raw and vulnerable, but they can take on and exude a new vitality and can be worked into charming additions to your home. When you purchase an unfinished piece, imagine the end result or final surface treatment, then work backward to create the depth and texture that will give the piece its character.

I purchased this unfinished pine dresser from a discount store that sells raw wood furniture. It was a sturdy, inexpensive piece filled with possibility. The treatment I selected is a simple aging process in which one color appears to have worn off through years of repeated handling, exposing the undercolor. The red and green I've chosen are complementary colors, found opposite each other on the color wheel. For a pleasing effect in a room setting, it's important to select paint colors that appeal to rather than jar the eye. The richness and subtlety of the surface treatment comes from the fact that the value, tone, and intensity of the two colors are similar. I studied color samples, then had one quart of each custom-mixed at my local hardware store.

I also replaced the original wooden knobs on the dresser drawers with some old cabinet hardware I found, upgrading the whole look of the piece. That simple finishing touch transformed the dresser, changing its personality and making it richer in appearance.

MATERIALS
sandpaper
steel wool
tack cloth
interior latex paint: barn red, hunter green
paintbrushes
scrub pad
sponge
Butcher's wax

1. Begin by removing the knobs and lightly sand dresser. Rub down with a fine steel wool for a smoother surface, then wipe down with tack cloth to remove sawdust and steel wool fibers. Paint entire surface with barn-red latex and allow to dry. Because this is new, unfinished wood, you'll need to apply a second coat.

2. Lightly sand dresser and wipe down with tack cloth. Paint entire surface with hunter-green latex and allow to dry.

3. Use a scrub pad and water to remove some of the green and reveal the red. Use a sponge to wipe off loosened paint, rinsing frequently in water. Work gently, following the grain of the wood, using long, horizontal strokes that relate to the surface of the piece. Open and close the drawers to note where your hands come in contact with the surface. You'll want to remove some paint from these areas so the piece will appear used and worn.

4. Stand back and evaluate your work from time to time. Does it look convincing? Too subtle? Step right up and remove some more green paint. When you've finally achieved the desired effect, wipe dresser free of surface debris and allow to dry. Use an application of Butcher's wax to seal and preserve the surface. Buff to a deep luster.

WICKER ROCKER I was initially attracted to this wicker rocker because of its terrific cranberry color, but I knew the color wasn't going to work in my home. It needed another color, another treatment to tone it down and class it up, allowing it to blend in and harmonize with the other furnishings. Rather than stripping the whole thing to bare wicker fiber and starting from scratch, I used the red color as the base and applied some gold latex eggshell-finish paint over it. I could have removed some of the red pigment with a water-soluble paint remover, revealing some of the natural wicker fiber. This would become part of the base, which could then be highlighted and enhanced.

After the gold paint had dried, I used a wet sponge to wipe some of it off and reveal the red. This finished rocker nicely complements the fabrics in its new environment.

A word of caution: If you put too much water on your sponge, the paint itself can absorb the water, and you could very easily wipe away all of the paint you've just applied. A delicate touch and the correct degree of moisture are required to give you a pleasing result. As with so many things, "less is more." Start with very little moisture and a delicate touch, adding moisture and pressure as needed. Stand back and assess the results of your labor while the surface is still wet, keeping in mind that's how it will look under a coat of polyurethane. Notice how comparatively flat and dull it looks when the surface dries.

You'll be much more comfortable with these processes and confident in your abilities once you have experimented with a couple of pieces.

Don't be discouraged if you feel you've made a mistake — it's easily correctable. Remember, you can always repeat the process of painting and scrubbing on areas where you may have fumbled.

This is a very simple and satisfying country finish that takes only a few hours to execute. Nonetheless, you want to allow sufficient time for the fiber you're working on to dry completely before you seal it. I sealed and finished the rocker with a coat of water-soluble polyurethane. It's easy to brush on, one application is sufficient, and I was able to wash out my brush in the kitchen sink.

MATERIALS
soap and water
vacuum with hose attachment
interior latex paint: gold, eggshell finish
paintbrush
combination kitchen sponge
water-based polyurethane
polyurethane brush

1. To prepare the surface, the whole rocker should be washed clean with a mild soap-and-water solution, wiped down, and thoroughly dried. Use your vacuum attachment to remove any debris from the weave. Coat the entire rocker in gold latex paint and allow to dry.

2. Use the scrub side of a kitchen sponge to remove much of the paint, exposing the red undercolor. Wipe off the loosened paint residue with the soft side of the sponge, rinsing frequently.

3. Allow at least 24 hours for any moisture locked within the fibers of the furniture to evaporate. Seal with one coat of water-soluble polyurethane.

SIDE TABLE This simple, early two-drawer side table is one of my favorite pieces. When I spotted it in the antique shop, I was immediately taken with its general character, the drawer construction, and the detail on the legs. They have a wonderful architectural quality about them — long, flat, angular planes, rings, cones, and spheres. Although architecture is a word that relates more to buildings than to furniture, every piece of furniture has its own distinct architectural elements, which make up its design.

What I've done with this table is accent its architecture. After application of an undercolor, or base coat, of barn red, the basic structure was articulated with green and yellow paint in a way that really points up the strength of the table's design and accents the linear composite of shapes that make up the leg. The basic difference between the treatment of the dresser on page 54 and the side table is the use of the third color, green, for accent and contrast.

MATERIALS
acrylic paint: barn red, mustard yellow, green
paintbrush
sandpaper
tack cloth
artist's brush
combination kitchen sponge
Butcher's wax

1. Prepare the surface for the undercoat by following the general instructions on page 26. Paint entire surface barn red and allow to dry. Lightly sand and wipe down with tack cloth. Paint surface with mustard-yellow acrylic; allow to dry.

2. Paint drawer faces, knobs, and leg details deep green. It would be awkward and somewhat difficult to use masking tape on the legs. Instead, use a small artist's brush and take your time.

3. Use a combination kitchen sponge and water to remove some of the green and yellow paint, revealing the red. Use the scrub side to loosen and the soft side to lift and remove loosened paint, rinsing frequently in water. Work gently, removing the paint in a way that makes the table appear timeworn.

4. When you've finally achieved the desired effect, allow to dry. Wipe down with tack cloth and apply Butcher's wax to seal and preserve the surface. Buff to a deep luster.

PAINT TEXTURES

Scumbling is a method of blending one or more colors in a smoky, dreamlike way, creating additional colors and depth in the blending process. This sounds more complicated than it is. It's actually a pretty easy technique that doesn't require a lot of paint or water. Scumbling is the application of separate, vaguely defined areas of paint, scuffing them up as you apply them so they billow across the surface. They should look hazy and translucent, not solid or opaque. You join these painted areas together while they are still wet to create a unified, textured background by using a stiff-bristled brush, pushing the paint from one area into another. This creates an undulation of dappled color on the surface, with gentle transitions from, say, peach to orange to gray, or whatever colors you've used. The more colors you apply, the greater the pulse of the surface. The beauty of a scumbled surface is its subtle complexity.

You can introduce some interesting details by scumbling. If you can make these soft patches of color blend together, you can also make them into a sky, or into textured rolling hills, or into variations of tree forms, for example. It's all within your reach and within your creative ability.

I applied random patches of color to the spotted box in the manner described above, but some interesting variations are possible. You could easily apply colors in soft-edged vertical or horizontal stripes or other patterns and still achieve that soft transition and blending between colors. You can create a rich assortment of surfaces, accentuating the undercolor, or covering it in some areas with a more opaque application of paint. You could master the technique of scumbling in an afternoon. The fun is going to last all of your creative days.

SPOTTED BOX When I found the box I used in this project (the one at the bottom in the picture at left), it was covered with layers of murky paint and residue. After it had been stripped, I decided to give it a coat of deep green latex with a lot of black in it. This formed a good base on which to apply lighter, warmer contrasting colors. One of the things you'll explore with this project is bringing the background color to the foreground, creating a surface rhythm of light and dark, warm and cool. The surface will take on a depth and pulse that's full of life and energy.

When you're painting a piece with an interior that will show when the piece is open, such as a box or an armoire, don't forget about the inside surfaces. Paint them a color, then rub it out with sandpaper or a sponge so it has a worn quality similar to the outside treatment. This completes the project, making the entire piece feel more authentic.

MATERIALS
interior latex paint: deep green
paintbrush
acrylic paint: warm earth colors, black
stiff-bristled artist's brush
scrub sponge
paper towels or clean rag
stencil brush
Butcher's wax

1. **Prepare surface of box and paint a base coat of deep green latex; allow to dry. Choose four warm color tones to contrast with the dark green base. On a palette or plate, squeeze out some of each color. Working on one side of the box at a time, ending with the top, use the stiff-bristled artist's brush in a jabbing or pouncing motion to form soft cloud shapes over the deep green base. It's essential the brush not have any excess moisture on it. If you wash the brush between color applications, make sure it is completely dry before moving on.**

Use this technique to apply clouds of the various colors, spacing them a few inches apart and going back into already painted areas to scrub and blend the shapes and colors together. This mushing around with the brush will not give you a solid or opaque surface, but a somewhat translucent one that will show the undercolor coming through. It's important to have that dark base peek out every once in a while.

After you have blended all of the earth-tone colors, allow them to dry. It will take just a moment, because they are very thin. If you're doing this out in the garden, as I did, you'll find they dry almost instantly; but give them a little time to set.

2. **When the paint is dry, use your lightly moistened scrub sponge and a circular motion to gently rub parts of the scumbled surface away, exposing the deep green undercolor. Wipe away the loosened bits of paint with a damp paper towel or rag. Allow to dry.**

3. Next, accent the surface with a series of irregular, randomly placed spots. To decide on an approximate pattern, make some sketches beforehand. You want this surface to have some spontaneity, but if you're not confident enough to go at it in a random, freehand way, you could plot out your spot pattern with light pencil lines.

Use your stencil brush or any flat-headed stiff-bristled brush about the size of your thumb in diameter. Again, keep the brush dry. Place a small amount of black paint in a cup or container, moisten the brush with the paint, then dab it on paper once or twice to remove excess paint before you apply it to your surface. This is important, for if the paint is too thick, you may ruin the scumbled undersurface trying to remove it. (If it's too thin, you can always go over it a second time.) Remember, a good carpenter always measures twice and cuts once.

Dab your stencil brush into the paint, then onto the box to create the dot pattern. Use enough pressure that the bristles flare and the edges of the spots are soft and irregular. Practice first on a piece of paper. You don't want this pattern to look like polka dots, but a random, rhythmic group of tiny explosions that complement the scumbled surface. If the spots seem too strong or prominent, soften them by lightly dabbing with a moistened rag or sponge to blur the edge. After spots are completely dry, finish with an application of Butcher's wax.

Stippling is a painting technique that creates wonderful textures. Where scumbling is a churning motion with the wrist and brush, stippling is the same pouncing motion you use to paint stencils; you're simply covering a larger surface using the same technique, rhythm, and motion. Color can be stippled onto a surface with a stencil brush or any stiff-bristled brush, or with a wad of cheesecloth or a gauze pad. Stippling creates a more interesting texture than a solid, opaque application of paint. Surface variations are created by using different pressures. A gentle pressure yields a lighter tone, a heavier hand will result in a darker tone. Light or dark results are also determined by the density of your stippling. Are you pouncing three times per square inch or twelve? Practice on newsprint to see the difference this makes.

You can go over a stippled area with another color, creating a more complex surface treatment. You can blend from one color into another by lightening your pressure and letting the colors visually dissolve into each other. One color can wash over another like a wave — light, darker, darkest. Everything is determined by that jabbing motion and its subtle variations, which take very little time to master. Once you get the feel for it, you can travel over large surface areas relatively quickly. "Traveling" is a good way to describe the process. Because your pouncing has become a rhythm, you must keep moving over the entire surface or you'll end up with dark areas. Feather the edges to create a consistent pattern.

Keep in mind that each time you reapply paint to your stipple brush, you must next blot it on a rag or paper towel. It's important to do this before going back to the surface you're painting so you don't create a mark that will be difficult to blend with the rest of the surface.

QUILT CHAIR This is a fun, casual, spirited chair. The inspiration for the painted treatment of this chair was a favorite quilt of mine. Almost any quilt pattern will do, and the design you transfer to the seat should be proportioned up or down so the painted "cushion" is a single, distinct panel, as I've done here. The chair was given a base coat of a putty color, and after the seat pattern was defined with masking tape, the other colors were stippled on. In a sense, I just filled in the other "blanks," applying colors to the back supports, rungs, back, legs, and so on.

The colors used on the chair reflect the colors of the quilt. You could change the entire palette, however, to fit your decor. Because of its recognizable pattern this design could be adapted to your kitchen chairs, creating the illusion of a seat cushion. Imagine a set of these chairs with a different quilt panel on each seat. A quilt pattern can be adapted to a set of barstools, a nightstand, a kitchen table, or to an individual chair that stands alone in a room. While it might not work in your living room or at your desk, it would be the perfect chair for a sewing room.

MATERIALS

interior latex paint: putty color

paintbrush

masking tape

straightedge

pencil

acrylic paint: gold, red, green, blue

stencil brush

painting tape

small artist's brush

water-based polyurethane

polyurethane brush

1, 2. Prepare surface (see page 26) and paint entire chair with a base coat of putty-color latex; allow to dry. On the seat, mask out a large square and then divide it into four smaller squares with tape. Using a straightedge to guide you, translate the pattern of the quilt onto the seat with a pencil.

3. Working with one color at a time, and starting with a clean, dry brush for each color, paint the various surfaces of the chair. Squeeze some acrylic paint onto a palette or plate. Dab the stencil brush into paint, then a few times onto some newsprint or a clean spot on the palette to blend the paint and avoid globs. Using a steady rhythm and pressure, stipple paint onto the surfaces with a gentle jabbing or pouncing motion.

4. Use painting tape (which is less likely than masking tape to pull up newly painted surfaces) to delineate the accents on the rungs. Stipple paint onto the accent areas and allow to dry. Remove the tape.

5. To paint the seat, paint outside corners of the quilt square gold and the rest of the seat outside the tape red. Lay painting tape down the long side of the inner triangles for a clean edge between the blue and gold. Paint the inner triangles blue and allow to dry. Remove the tape and use a small artist's brush to hand paint the areas now exposed green. When chair is completely dry, seal with two coats of water-soluble polyurethane.

The sea sponge is a versatile tool used to apply paint, to remove paint, and to blend colors on a surface, among other uses. Sponging is really a lot of fun, and it's very easy to do. It doesn't require much explanation, and the best way to learn the technique is simply to practice creating textures by dabbing paint on some newsprint. Use a dessert or dinner plate as your palette; dip the sponge into a small amount of paint and dab or blot the sponge on a clean area of the plate before dabbing it on paper. Once you feel comfortable making a uniform pattern on the newsprint, transfer the same process to some scrap wood. The wood will feel different than the paper, and the result will more closely approximate your final surface.

The sponging process is very much like stippling in that it involves a rhythmic pouncing motion. Travel evenly over the entire surface with the sponge — several times if necessary to achieve the desired degree of coverage. If you work on too small an area at first, you'll have difficulty making it blend with the rest of the surface. Strive for a light touch to produce a consistently textured pattern and an even density of color.

Because sea sponges are a natural product, their fiber texture varies, so when purchasing sponges (you'll find them at bath shops or hardware stores) look at them carefully and choose between an open, porous texture or a fine, dense texture. Or get them both. They'll produce different results. Sometimes sea sponges are sold in bags, offering a variety of sizes and textures. You don't want to come home with the wrong sponge, so be sure to examine them prior to your purchase.

Cut off a small piece of sponge to paint inner corners and other hard-to-reach places. It's important to go back to your practice surface first, though, because when you reduce the size of the sponge, you also need to adjust your dabbing pressure to maintain the consistency of the developing pattern.

Sponging can be used to apply a distinct, high-contrast pattern over a base color, as with the blue and ochre or red and ochre on the linen press (page 92). You can also create a much denser, richer texture with a sponge by choosing a monochromatic palette — maybe several shades of green — or a palette containing colors of similar saturation and value (ivory and pale pink over white, for example). You can really blend colors with a sea sponge. Many variations can be created with this one tool. Notice the different character of the child's chair (page 119) compared to the linen press.

As with most country finish techniques you'll explore, take your time, proceeding slowly at first, then watch your confidence and skills increase. Have fun.

HICKORY SET This set of hickory furniture had once been painted. It was also quite weathered and was in need of repair. Even weathered and broken, these pieces had a handsome strength and simplicity, and needed only a little attention to bring them back to a functional state. Two broken struts were replaced, and while the woven seat could have been salvaged, I chose instead a simpler solution and replaced the seat with heavy-duty canvas, folding over the end and stapling it to the new struts. This was done after the painted surface was sealed.

I chose to simply heighten rather than alter the existing texture and color of these hickory pieces with a sponged paint treatment. To soften the seat, I added upholstered pillows, which were attached with twelve-inch ties. The cushions are reversible, beige on one side, white on the other, allowing for some decorative versatility. These cushions really dressed up the whole set, making it as appropriate inside a home as it once was on a summer porch.

This is a country finish you could easily do in an afternoon. Hickory furniture, or, for that matter, any rustic sort of "twig" furniture, is ideal for this sort of treatment, because the natural texture of the sponge complements the bark of the wood. This simple and subtle treatment elevates these pieces from the ordinary to the sophisticated.

MATERIALS
sponge
large rag
acrylic paint: white, beige
sea sponge
acrylic spray sealer
white canvas
staple gun

1. Rub the pieces down with a moist sponge then a large rag; allow to dry. Using white acrylic paint and a sea sponge, dab over the structure of the furniture in a random way and allow to dry. Using a clean, dry sponge, repeat this process with the beige acrylic paint. Use the white paint first to brighten the piece, then tone it down to a more muted shade with the beige.

2. When all paint is dry, spray surface of structure with a clear acrylic sealer.

3. Staple white canvas across horizontal supports to create seat.

TRUNK I found this nicely constructed antique trunk while browsing through a local shop. Its interesting hardware caught my eye, and closer inspection revealed it was signed on the bottom by its maker or owner. The trunk was painted a deep green but was badly scarred by a solvent that had been spilled on it. Because of this, I stripped it down to bare wood, being careful to retain the signature. I also left the hardware in its original state.

In the following project, the sponge was used to create an all-over texture on the sides and front of the linen press. The sponge was used in a couple of different ways on the trunk. Swiping and dabbing created cometlike shapes on the sides, and the tree shapes in the scumbled landscape on top were developed using a couple of different sea sponges.

The top of the trunk was plotted out on paper to create the folk-inspired landscape, a reflection of early painting treatments that frequently appear on antique chests and other furniture. The background was painted using sponges to wash the surface with different colors, creating the mountains and sky. The trees were developed by using the sponge in a vertical continuous way, or on its side to form the boughs of the pine trees or the trees themselves. There are a number of different tree shapes, and each shape was developed by using the sponge and its various sides.

MATERIALS

steel wool

tack cloth

acrylic paint: terra-cotta, ochre, black, white, blue,
   shades of green, clay color, brown

sea sponge

paintbrush

combination kitchen sponge

Butcher's wax

1. Strip the trunk and prepare surface for new paint by rubbing down with a medium then a fine grade of steel wool. Wipe clean with tack cloth. Using the sponge and a terra-cotta shade of acrylic paint, freely apply slashes on the four sides of the trunk. Remember to blot your sponge each time you reapply paint to it. Gently strike the surface in an arcing left-to-right and right-to-left pattern. Allow to dry. Wash the sponge and wring it out, then randomly apply some additional swipes of ochre on top of the terra-cotta strokes.

2. When the ochre has dried, use black acrylic to accent the painted slashes. This piling up of color on the cometlike shape will create an overall texture with an early, primitive simplicity. Turn the sponge and gently apply black paint to create an additional texture over the trunk surface. Wash the sponge again.

3. Use the sponge to create a simple, idealized landscape on the trunk lid. Paint the upper half white and blue for sky, and the bottom half a few shades of light green for pastures and hills. Use a darker green to add mountains on the horizon, and define the road with a clay color. Gently scumble the paint onto the surface in a way that allows some of the character of the wood to show through. Develop the tree shapes by sponging on a light green, then sponge over a darker shade to further define them. Use your paintbrush to paint trunks and boughs brown.

4. Once the paint is completely dry, use the abrasive side of a moistened kitchen sponge to remove or "erase" some of the painted designs; wipe off loose paint with cellulose side of sponge, rinsing sponge frequently. Scuffing up the surface will help convey an appearance of age. When completely dry, wipe clean with tack cloth, apply a coat of amber Butcher's wax, and buff to a low luster.

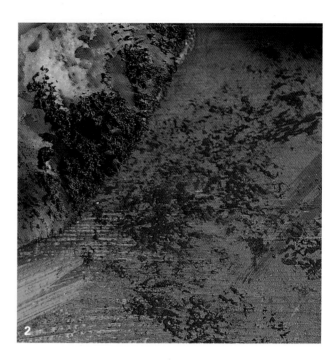

LINEN PRESS I found this two-door cabinet with an existing color treatment that didn't work in the environment I purchased it for. I liked the segregation of color on the different components of the cabinet, however, and decided to do a fresh surface treatment with a sea sponge. This is an extremely simple project.

I tested three color combinations on the back of the cabinet before deciding on the final ones. The top is painted solid red, which gives the piece a certain boldness and strength. Blue dominates the body of the cabinet. Over that blue is a dark ochre, which reduces the intensity of the blue. The inset panel was painted ochre; red was sponged over it to reduce its intensity and to complement the solid red of the top. These shades bring in the range of colors from the room environment and blend nicely within the piece. I went beyond the palette of blue, red, and ochre, using green to define the inset detail on the door panel.

In applying paint with the sponge, travel over the entire surface using a broad and circular flowing motion so you aren't left with hard lines or defined shapes. You can go back over the surface to make a more dense pattern if you like. It's important to continually reapply paint to your sponge and to blot it out to evenly distribute the paint before you touch the sponge back on your surface.

MATERIALS

interior latex paint: blue, ochre, red, green
paintbrush
sea sponge
artist's brush
Butcher's wax

1. Prepare the surface (see page 26) and paint cabinet dark blue, paint inset door panels ochre, and paint top red. Allow to dry.

2. For the sponging process, use a large enough surface or palette to moisten your sponge with paint; I like to use an old dinner plate or bowl. Make sure the paint is evenly distributed on the sponge before you apply it to the surface. If there's too much paint on the sponge, you're going to create globs that disrupt the pattern. Practice the technique and experiment with color combinations and pattern density on an unseen area first. Dip the sea sponge into some red paint on a palette or plate and blot it around the palette. Sponge over the ochre panels on the doors in a random pattern; allow to dry. Thoroughly wash and dry sea sponge, then use ochre paint to cover the blue body of the cabinet.

3. Use an artist's brush and green paint to accent the inset border on the doors. Allow to dry, wipe clean of debris, then finish the piece with an application of clear Butcher's wax.

DECORATIVE SHELF

One of the items in the picture at left is a decorative little shelf I discovered in an antique store. Its scale and symmetrical proportions are very charming. What especially interested me when I first spotted it was the incised grooves making up the attractive design on the vertical surface. I became more interested in it when I saw the price, so I took it home to apply a new finish.

This accessory has the kind of character that lends itself to any number of treatments. I chose to give it a somewhat unusual color treatment and texture by using a high-contrast combination of colors — a warm, ochre base, or undercolor, sponged over with black. The design inspiration came from the lidded, cylindrical boxes you see on the finished shelf. They were purchased in the desert in Pakistan many years ago, and I have always admired their texture. By using a finely textured sea sponge, I was able to give the shelf a surface that reflected those boxes.

MATERIALS

acrylic paint: warm ochre, black

paintbrushes

sea sponge

water-based polyurethane

polyurethane brush

1. Prepare the surface (see page 26) and use a brush to apply base coat of deep, warm ochre. Allow to dry and add a second coat. Once the base color has dried completely, use a sea sponge with fine pores to sponge black paint over the entire surface of the shelf. Be sure to blot the sponge on your palette or some newsprint before you apply it to the shelf, to avoid blobs.

2. Hard-to-reach inside corners can be painted by using a small piece of sponge cut from a larger one.

3. Use a small paintbrush or watercolor brush to define incised lines with ochre paint.

4. When all paint has dried, cover with a protective coat of water-based polyurethane. This finish is preferable because it would be unnecessarily difficult to buff Butcher's wax from those inside corners. Apply the polyurethane with a small brush to coat those areas more easily.

DECORATIVE TECHNIQUES

Hand painting brings a certain folksy, informal feel to a piece of furniture, and will give the surface a unique vitality and character.

Handpainted details can make a piece very special. Small, regularly spaced freehand dots or diamonds created with a stencil brush or flat-tipped artist's brush can add a jaunty, friendly quality to a piece of stained or painted furniture. Add handpainted tendrils to your stenciled grape leaves, or red berries around your ivy stencil.

Practice first on newsprint or some scrap wood. You may want to lightly outline your design in pencil. You can stay within the lines by using a smaller brush to do an outline, then fill in with a larger brush. If you go outside a line, don't panic. Since you're working with acrylic paints, you can take a damp rag or paper towel and scuff from the edge of the mistake back into the outlined area and move on. Don't be afraid to go outside those lines a little bit, because you don't want your handpainted design to look as rigid as a coloring book.

To steady your hand, you can hold the brush low, near the bristles, and rest the heel of your hand on the vertical or horizontal surface that you're painting. You can approach it from any direction — side, top, or bottom — that will help you feel comfortably anchored and in control.

If you're painting a line on a surface, you can approach it mechanically, using masking tape to segregate the divisions of color, or use your hand. Freehand painting is going to yield very different results than stenciling or masking. Handpainted lines will have a softer and more wobbly edge, and you should consider this when planning your design. The subtle variations of the handpainted line may be more reflective of an older style of painted furniture — softer, more reflective or personal, and probably much more desirable. The element of personality is important, and hand painting really gives a piece distinctive qualities.

PLAID BOX Here's another hand painting project. In this instance I began with a found hinged box (the long, open box in the photograph at left) and freehand painted it a plaid pattern. Its color inspiration came from a piece of antique Indonesian batik, and the way the plaid design was applied mimics the woven character of an old kitchen tablecloth or dishtowel. A red rectangle painted around the keyhole adds color and visual interest, and a darker line applied to the right and bottom of the rectangle fools the eye and creates depth.

Once all the paint had dried, I covered the box in an antiquing mixture. It's available premixed in a number of shades from craft stores. It gives the box a sort of dirty look, creating a pretty convincing illusion of genuine age. You could also opt to forego the antiquing solution and keep the box clean. Remember, you have choices for variations with all these processes. Sometimes genius and success are about knowing just when to stop.

This is really a weekend project, requiring roughly a day for preparation and priming and an afternoon or evening to apply the plaid design, the antiquing solution (two hours after paint dries), and Butcher's wax.

MATERIALS
screwdriver
sandpaper
tack cloth
sponge brush
acrylic paint: white (primer coat), putty color, blue,
    black, red
graph paper
pencil
ruler or T-square
1/4-inch and 1/2-inch artist's brushes, short-bristled
    and flat-tipped
masking tape
combination kitchen sponge
water-soluble antiquing
paintbrush
Butcher's wax

1. **Remove latches and handles from top and sides (these are not replaced). Lightly sand box to break the surface and make it ready for paint. Wipe clean with tack cloth. Using a sponge brush, paint box inside and out with a primer coat of white acrylic and allow to dry. Paint the outside surface of the box with putty-color acrylic and allow to dry. This will be your base coat.**

2. Plot out a plaid design on graph paper, then lightly transfer it to the surface of the box with pencil, using a ruler or T-square as a straightedge. Take the time to carefully work out this stage. It's easier to plan a few designs and see how they work on paper than to repaint the box.

Mix some blue and black acrylic paint to the desired deep shade. Using your 1/2-inch and 1/4-inch artist's brushes, follow the pencil line with the paintbrush, stippling or dabbing horizontally across the pencil line. Use a consistent pouncing motion, rhythm, and pressure. Practice the technique first on some scrap paper. Which lines you paint with which brush will determine the widths of the lines and the character of the pattern. Paint over all the pencil lines. Use the blue you've mixed and the sponge brush to paint the inside of the box as well. Allow to dry.

Use masking tape to create a rectangle around keyhole. Paint red, allow to dry. With the cellulose side of a kitchen sponge, sponge black over red and when dry, use the rough side of the sponge to scuff the surface to further tone it down. Wipe off loosened particles with damp sponge. Paint a black outline along the bottom and right side of the rectangle.

3. When paint is completely dry, brush on water-soluble brown antiquing mixture, thoroughly covering the entire outside surface of the box. When the mixture has set, use a very damp sponge to take most of it away. What remains in the cracks and crevices of the wood gives a convincing illusion of age and blends the colors in a more unified way. When box is completely dry, finish it with an application of Butcher's wax and buff to a low-luster sheen. You've now sealed the box with a great-looking old patina and finish, and it's ready to use.

TWIG TABLE This is a straightforward country finish project that could easily be completed in a single day.

I discovered this unique twig table in its old, dark, natural state at a neighbor's yard sale. I painted it an apple-sap green to give it a whole new character and vitality. It says, "Look at me!" and calls attention to its natural structure and presence within a room.

I wanted the tabletop to have a Pennsylvania Dutch or quiltlike quality, and experimented with some cutout paper shapes before I arrived at this simple folk-inspired design. I cut out four curved shapes and some small triangles and moved them around in various configurations — much the same way one might make drawings. I encourage you to try this approach. Play directly with a surface prior to committing it to paint and see what kind of design best fits its shape and character. Sometimes you can get a better feel for what a finished piece will look like using this method as opposed to making drawings.

I had to go back and repaint one area because I had scrubbed away too much of the design. The beauty of acrylic paint is that mistakes are easily correctable. All they cost you is a little time, and they can teach you something in the process.

MATERIALS

soap and water

interior latex paint: bright green

paintbrush

combination kitchen sponge

paper

masking tape

acrylic paint: ochre, black, terra-cotta

artist's brush

Butcher's wax

1. Prepare surface with a thorough washdown with soap and water. Wipe down and allow to dry. Starting with table upside down, paint entire surface bright green. Allow to dry and recoat for total coverage. Once paint has dried, use moistened scrubber sponge to remove paint from areas where it would naturally have worn off through repeated handling over a period of time. Wipe off loosened paint with cellulose side of sponge, rinsing sponge frequently, and allow table to dry. Cut out paper templates and move them around on the tabletop until you are satisfied with the arrangement of shapes.

2. Double-check the relative placements of the templates with a ruler and secure them to the tabletop with masking tape. Pencil lightly around the edges of the templates to transfer the pattern to the tabletop.

3. Remove templates, and use acrylic paints and a medium-sized artist's brush to paint within the lines you've drawn.

4. When paint is dry, use rough side of kitchen sponge to remove some of the design, once again following the process of scrubbing and wiping.

5. Remove loosened paint with soft side of kitchen sponge and allow table to dry. Finish with a coating of amber Butcher's wax to add a subtle darkening to the surface. Buff to a deep luster.

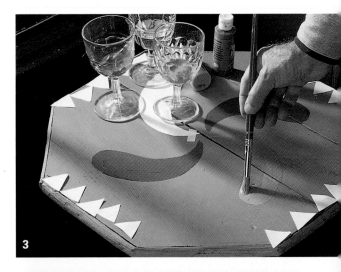

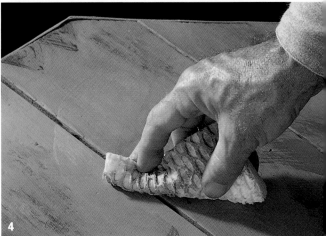

When you want to add a personal statement to a piece of furniture, stenciling and combing are easy and satisfying. The simple techniques involved in applying a combing treatment are described on page 110. There are a large variety of precut stencils available from art supply stores, mail order companies, and the like, many of which reflect primitive Early American border patterns, simple geometric designs, or landscape elements such as fruits, flowers, and trees. It's not a difficult process, however, to adapt a design you like into your own custom stencil — perhaps something you like in a magazine. As long as you can draw or trace the image onto a sheet of paper, you can enlarge or reduce it as much as you like using a photocopy machine. You can also turn your own freehand drawings into a stencil that more closely reflects your personal taste and style.

There are two different types of stencil paper available; one is translucent, the other opaque. I don't recommend the opaque variety. I prefer the see-through quality of the translucent paper.

Use tracing paper or drawing paper to trace or create an image. I sometimes find it's helpful to tape the image I'm about to trace onto a window, where I can tape the stencil paper directly over it and draw on the stencil paper itself, saving a step. Let's assume you're using tracing paper, however. Outline the image heavily with a dark marker or soft pencil, then secure with tape to a good cutting surface — an artist's cutting mat is perfect, but some heavy cardboard or the back of a drawing pad will do nicely. You could also work directly on a kitchen cutting board. You should not cut directly on a counter or table surface, however, because you can easily damage the surface with your knife. Tape the stencil paper over the darkly outlined image and carefully cut it out with a razor knife or sharp utility knife.

Of the three stenciling projects we're going to show you, only one was created using a purchased stencil. An original handcut design was used on the other two projects. The game board on Arthur's bench, however, was applied with the help of a purchased precut stencil, many of which are made of durable plastic and come in a variety of sizes.

The painting motion is a simple pouncing with a stencil brush. Stenciling is a genuinely fun surface treatment, particularly for beginners. Soon you'll find you're having such a good time that you'll have to restrain yourself from going off the piece of furniture you're working on, up the walls, over the doors, and into the next room. Stenciling is so enjoyable because your efforts are rewarded immediately. The possibilities for creative stenciling are limited only by your imagination.

GRAPE LEAF CHAIR This chair had beautiful proportions but was visually weighed down by its black stain. My goal was to lighten the color and give the chair a timeworn appearance. Some of the original surface has been retained in this treatment, incorporating the old with the new. I like to do that whenever I can.

Using a scrub sponge, I went down through two layers of newly applied paint to reveal some of the black stain. The result is subtle yet complex, and the treatment looks more than skin deep. There's a mystery and depth about the new finish that invites visual exploration; it seems to pull the eye into the chair itself rather than allowing it to simply travel across or rest upon the surface.

I wanted the stencil accents to reflect an element of nature, and went looking around the yard for some interesting leaf shapes with the right proportions. Deciding on grape leaves, I removed a section of vine from the grape arbor and brought it indoors to develop a stencil.

This is very easy to do, and like an elegant but simple dessert, impresses people every time. Use a few leaves, ferns, sprigs of ivy, or other flat, natural shapes that appeal to you. A photocopy machine can reduce or enlarge any image, so you don't have to spend a lot of time searching for an exact proportion. If you want to stencil some tiny leaves as an accent, just put the leaf shape you've chosen on the photocopier and use the reduce function. Even office technology can be used in some pretty creative ways.

MATERIALS

sandpaper

tack cloth

sponge brush

interior latex paint: gray-blue

soft-bristled brush

acrylic paint: white, shades of green, ochre

abrasive scrubbing pad

kitchen sponge

masking tape

leaves

tracing paper

dark pencil or marker

stencil paper

razor knife

stencil brush

artist's brush

Butcher's wax or water-based polyurethane

1. Prepare the surface by sanding lightly, then rubbing down with tack cloth. Use a sponge brush to paint chair with a gray-blue latex base coat and allow to dry. Using a soft-bristled brush, scumble white acrylic paint mixed with a small amount of latex base color over the chair. Move the brush swiftly over the surface to create an irregular texture. Allow the gray-blue base color to show through to dominate certain areas, while the opaque white dominates in others. This will give the chair its initial base texture. Allow to dry.

2. Use an abrasive scrubbing pad to remove some paint from the surface of the chair, revealing the original black stain.

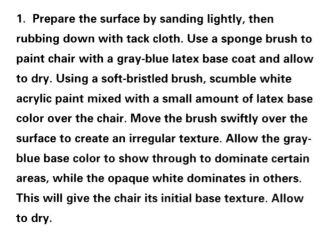

3. Use kitchen sponge and paper toweling to lift and remove loosened paint.

4. To create the stencil, tape the leaves you've chosen to some white paper. Trace an outline of the leaf shape on the paper with dark pencil. Remove the leaf, tape a sheet of translucent stencil paper over your tracing, and secure with tape.

5. Using a razor knife, carefully cut around the pencil tracing to free the paper leaf. You can cut several leaf shapes out of a single piece of stencil paper. To decide where to apply the stencil, use masking tape to position the real leaves in various places on the chair. Experiment a bit; move things around, then stand back to determine what you want. These design decisions can be made without using paint. When you've settled on a design, tape the stencil into place.

5

6. Use a stencil brush to mix three or four acrylic colors on your palette; the back of an old plate will do nicely. I used a few different shades of green and a muted ochre. Make sure the stencil is flush with the surface, then blot your brush and dab some paint onto the chair surface. You can begin to mix colors as you dab one color over the other. Repeat this process for each stencil placement. The result is a spontaneous, natural-looking application.

6

7. Mix a new color for the leaf stems or grapevine itself, and apply freehand with a soft artist's brush. Experiment on paper first, or make a faint pencil line on the chair to guide you. I made a gesture with my hand that indicated the essence of the stem. I then accentuated it with little curls that reflect the tendrils of the vine in an adaptation or interpretation of nature. When the paint is completely dry, seal finish with either an application of Butcher's wax or water-based polyurethane.

ARTHUR'S BENCH

This newly constructed pine bench was copied from an antique in my friend Arthur's home. I was immediately attracted to the old, classically shaped bench because of its nice proportions. My contribution to its design was the addition of a removable shelf painted as a game board.

This project illustrates a handy shortcut using masking tape. The painted borders around the bench top and game board were created without the aid of a ruler, pencil, or straightedge. Instead, the width of the tape itself served as the measurement and guide.

First I laid long strips of tape even with the edge of the wood to define the outer edge of the border. Then I placed small pieces of masking tape — about 1/2 inch long — around the perimeter at roughly 6-inch intervals, flush with the outside strips of tape. They served as guides for the placement of long strips that would define the inner edge of the border. I then removed the short pieces of tape to reveal an evenly masked field in which to paint. A nice detail was created where the tape crossed at the corners, but you could prepare to paint an unbroken border by cutting through those intersections with a razor knife.

I cut some crescent-shaped stencils and applied them in gold and black in a random pattern on the bench top. You could plan out the pattern more carefully or use different shapes — stars, perhaps. As I discussed with the twig table on page 94, you can experiment with variations by cutting and placing paper shapes to help you find what's most pleasing to your eye.

The surface of the entire bench and game board was given two coats of water-soluble polyurethane. This is a more practical finish than Butcher's wax for pieces that will be used in casual environments or around children. Its harder surface will stand up to use and can be wiped clean with mild soap and water.

MATERIALS
sandpaper
tack cloth
interior latex paint: hunter green
paintbrush
masking tape
acrylic paint: light green, black, gold
stencil brush
dark pencil or marker
paper
stencil paper
razor knife
ruler
precut checkerboard stencil
water-soluble polyurethane
polyurethane brush

1. Prepare surface by lightly sanding and rubbing down with tack cloth. Paint entire bench and both sides of shelf a deep hunter green latex and allow to dry. Sand surfaces lightly, wipe with tack cloth, and apply second coat. When completely dry, define borders on bench top and shelf/game board with masking tape, following sequence described above. Apply light green acrylic paint inside the masked lines with your stencil brush, using the pouncing motion discussed earlier.

2. Draw some curved, crescent shapes on drawing or tracing paper. Outline darkly with soft pencil or marker. Secure with tape to an appropriate cutting surface, then tape translucent stencil paper on top of it. Cut shapes out with a razor knife or sharp utility knife. Randomly apply stencils in black and gold to bench surface within established border. Paint the black ones first, clean and dry your brush, and paint in the gold ones.

3. Use a ruler and masking tape to position and secure precut checkerboard stencil to shelf. Use stencil brush and gold paint; allow to dry. Once fully dry, reposition the stencil and paint remaining squares black. When all surfaces are completely dry, wipe free of debris and apply two coats of water-soluble polyurethane.

SMALL ARMOIRE I've had this lightly stained pine armoire in my home for many years, and finally decided to liven it up with a painted treatment. It had a surface coating of wax, which I removed.

There are a variety of colors in the palette I chose for this piece. The armoire was painted three coats of diluted blue paint in different shades. Prior to stenciling, there was a lot of wiping down and wiping away of color in an effort to create a surface with depth and age. The process of paint over paint is sometimes called a wash.

I applied blue paint to the entire piece except the drawer and inset panels of the doors, which were painted a cream color and, in the case of the door panels, were framed in barn red. This accented the architecture, or design, of the piece and visually lifted the panels of the structure.

MATERIALS

steel wool

tack cloth

acrylic paint: blues, greens, cream, barn red, gold, beige, salmon, cranberry

paintbrush

combination kitchen sponge

masking tape

stencil paper

pencil

razor knife

stencil brush

artist's brush

Butcher's wax

1. **Lightly steel wool the entire piece and rub down with tack cloth. Paint all but inset panels and drawer with three coats of diluted blue acrylic, starting with the lightest shade first. Use a damp combination kitchen sponge to scrub away and wipe off some of the painted layers. Once dry, paint the frame of the inset panel barn red. Paint inset panels and drawer a cream color. Scrub and wipe as before. Scumble a wash of green and dark blue on the sides of the armoire and then the inset panels of the doors to add some texture and disrupt the evenness of the surface. Allow to dry.**

Tape sheets of stencil paper over the left inset door panels and left side of the armoire and draw a series of simplified oak leaves and stems. Remove the paper to a suitable surface for cutting and with a razor knife cut out the stencil shapes.

2. Tape stencils in place on left door panels and side. Using an old dinner plate as your palette, put small amounts of different shades of green, gold, and beige on the plate. Dab into the paint with a stencil brush, blot your brush, and apply paint to the stencil; add additional colors while the paint is wet to create variations in the leaf. Turn the stencils and repeat the process on the right panels and side.

3. When stenciled designs have dried, use an artist's brush to hand paint tendrils with a couple of shades of green that echo nature. Paint berries one shade of red, then heighten with a lighter or darker shade (I used salmon and cranberry colors). Seal with a coat of clear Butcher's wax.

FARM TABLE For this piece I've used an old folk surface treatment known as combing. This is a process involving the manipulation of an overcolor. While the overcolor is still wet, you simply drag a comb across the surface to reveal the base color and create primitive-looking grains or patterns.

You can purchase metal or plastic combs in art supply stores, or make your own. Using stiff cardboard or plastic and a pair of scissors, you can cut "combs" to establish many different patterns simply by varying the intervals between cuts.

For the farm table, I cut a 4-inch square from the cardboard back of a legal pad, then cut a simple repeated V pattern on one side and snipped off the points, blunting the tips. The comb was dragged over wet blue paint to reveal the undercolor in the illustrated patterns: a grid for the legs, made by alternating a single horizontal and then vertical pass with the comb, and a running wave for the drawer and side panels. Illustrated are additional pattern possibilities. Have fun with them, and experiment with some of your own patterns.

MATERIALS
interior latex paint: putty color
paintbrush
cardboard
scissors
acrylic paint: blue, black
cheesecloth
Butcher's wax

1. After surface preparation (see page 26), completely paint the surface of the table with a beige or putty-color latex paint and allow to dry. Apply second coat and allow to dry thoroughly. Cut a 4-inch square of stiff cardboard — perhaps from a shirt that's come back from the cleaner's — then cut a sawtooth or V pattern on two sides. On one of the sides you've just cut, blunt the "teeth" by cutting off the very tips. You now have a combing tool that will create two different patterns or textures when raked or pulled through the wet overcolor. Experiment with creating patterns on a piece of paper or scrap wood. You can combine them on the same piece. Note the grid pattern on the table legs, for example.

2. Mix blue and black acrylic paint to the desired deep shade, and apply with paintbrush to the flat surfaces of the table.

3. Drag the comb through the freshly applied paint in the desired pattern. Work small areas, so that if you're not pleased with the combed pattern you can easily run your wet paintbrush over the surface, "erasing" the previous pattern, and try again. Because of the speedy drying time of acrylic paint, however, you must work somewhat quickly once you've painted the blue overcolor. If you paint too large an area and that blue paint dries, you'll have to start over with the base color.

4. Wad up a ball of cheesecloth. Dip into blue paint, blot on your palette or some newspaper, and lightly dab the cheesecloth onto the round turned elements of the leg and drawer pulls to give them a soft and subtle coloration. When all the paint has dried, finish with an application of clear Butcher's wax.

Different motions of the hand will create a wide variety of patterns. Experiment until you find one that suits the piece you are finishing.

Decoupage is the process of applying cutout paper illustrations, documents, photographs, or bits of fabric to a surface, then sealing them under multiple coats of lacquer or varnish. Our updated weekend approach to decoupage uses white glue, and replaces the varnish with four coats or so of quick-drying water-soluble polyurethane, yielding the same look as an antique decoupage treatment in a fraction of the time and without any unpleasant fumes or dangerous solvents.

Decoupage pieces often have a playful character and can be fun to plan. You might decoupage an old map and some postcards on a man's bureau; or some wallpaper swatches, children's drawings, or illustrations from a seed catalog on a kitchen table; perhaps even add some memorabilia from a family vacation to a bed tray. Other decoupage pieces could take a more classical decorative approach; imagine a beautiful little box with gold leaf accents featuring a historical architectural drawing on its lid. There's no shortage of possibilities or resources.

MIRRORED CABINET
The little mirrored cabinet used in this project was encrusted with several layers of paint when I found it at a local flea market. I've done an easy weekend treatment that features a combination of pickling, stenciling, and decoupage. Because I've decided to begin with a pickled base rather than a painted one, the cabinet had to be stripped down to the raw wood. The pickling process is explained in detail on page 128.

I've also used some great Victorian-style paper cutouts I found in an antique shop. I didn't know what I'd do with them at the time, but I thought they were charming and purchased them. They seemed to be the right sort of thing to apply to this lighthearted little cabinet. This kind of piece is perfect for a less formal environment, like a guest bathroom or a summer cottage.

MATERIALS
stripper
sandpaper
steel wool
tack cloth
acrylic paint: white, yellow, green, blue
wide flat-bristled brush
precut checkerboard stencil
masking tape or painting tape
stencil brush
paper cutouts
white glue
artist's brush
water-based polyurethane
sponge brush

1. Strip paint and prepare surface for pickling with sandpaper, steel wool, and tack cloth. Put a dab of white acrylic paint on a plate and add a small amount of water to dilute the paint.

2. Using a wide flat-bristled or sponge brush, gently apply this wash over the surface of the cabinet in the direction of the grain. It will penetrate and lighten the wood but will allow the wood grain to show through. When dry, repeat process a second time to lighten the surface further. Allow to dry.

3. Secure precut checkerboard stencil to surface with tape. Using a stencil brush and some yellow acrylic paint, stencil the whole surface and allow to dry.

4. Tentatively arrange your cutout images over the cabinet, taping them lightly into place before choosing a final design.

5. When you're pleased with the placement of the cutouts, turn them over one at a time and use an artist's brush to apply a solution of white glue mixed with a little water on the back, making sure to coat the edges. Press the glued images into place and allow to dry for at least 30 minutes. Place checkerboard stencil on surface again, carefully aligning it with the previously painted pattern. Taking color cues from the paper foliage, paint over some of the yellow squares with soft greens and blues and allow to dry. Lightly sand the painted areas to remove some color and make the surface appear aged. Wipe with tack cloth.

6. Using a sponge brush, apply satin-finish polyurethane to the entire surface and allow to dry. Repeat this final process until everything is securely embedded — about four coats should do it.

CHILD'S CHAIR This old Empire child's chair was found in an antique shop, cloaked in several layers of paint that obliterated its subtle carved surface details. The chair was badly in need of stripping, and was taken down to bare wood using Woodfinisher's Pride. Our chair is predominantly gray and blue, but you can choose any colors you'd like. Think about the favorite colors of the child it's intended for, or about the colors of the room it will be in.

This project is similar to the preceding one in that it reflects a combination of techniques and processes: a painted surface involving sponging, hand painting, and applied cutouts, or decoupage.

MATERIALS

interior latex paint: blue-gray

paintbrush

acrylic paint: turquoise for base coat; shades of green, blue, white for landscape background; various other colors for painted details

sponge

masking tape

gold spray paint

artist's brush

paper cutouts

white glue

water-based polyurethane

polyurethane brush

1. After stripping (see page 27 for technique), paint entire surface of chair with a latex primer coat — in this case, a light gray-blue — and allow to dry. Once dry, sponge on some acrylic turquoise, giving a depth and texture to the whole structure of the chair.

2. Use masking tape to define the accents on the legs and back supports, then spray with metallic gold paint. Whenever using spray paint, it's important to work with good ventilation, preferably outdoors. Use newspaper to protect the rest of the chair and floor around it from overspray.

3. Create the scene on the chair back by dividing the space into a series of little hills painted in shades of green. Paint the sky blue and allow to dry. Add clouds by scumbling with white paint. Hand paint trees with an artist's brush. When the paint is completely dry, arrange the paper cutouts on the chair back and seat and gently tape them into place. Attach cutouts to the painted surface with diluted white glue, using an artist's brush to completely coat the back of the cutout; pay particular attention to the edges. When glue has dried, touch up landscape with artist's brush.

4. When completely dry, apply water-based polyurethane to the entire surface, with additional coats on the chair back and seat. Because this chair is intended for a child, it's important to seal the paper cutouts under enough coats of polyurethane so that a child cannot pick or peel them off.

Historically, gold leaf and silver leaf were used to ornament paintings, frames, furniture, and interiors. Their use denoted opulence, elegance, and wealth.

All of the precious metals are available in leaf form, and they are, as one might guess, somewhat expensive. Imitation gold leaf, commonly referred to as Dutch metal, is sold in art and craft supply stores and is an economical substitute that allows you to treat ordinary objects in a playful way. The "leaves" are very thin 5-inch squares that require careful handling to minimize tearing. You can gild something like the ballroom chair used in the next project for a fraction of what it would cost to do it in pure metal, yet create a very rich appearance.

Gold leaf is affixed to a surface in a number of ways. You can purchase an adhesive specifically created for imitation gold leaf, like Rolco Quick-Dry Synthetic Gold Size Varnish, or you can use white glue.

Gold leafing can enhance shelves, small boxes, lamp bases, or picture frames. You can use Dutch metal to gold leaf unexpected objects like a twig table, totally changing their character. Highlight elements of chairs, tables, or other components within a room.

BALLROOM CHAIR
Traditionally, gold leaf was applied over a base color of terracotta or barn red. I've chosen to use a deep, almost cobalt shade of blue for this ballroom chair, but it could also have been a deep green. Choose any color you wish, but keep in mind that some of the gold leaf will brush off, and the complementary base color that's revealed should be an appropriately rich, deep tone.

I also used some Treasure Copper, a metallic paste available at art supply stores, to create additional contrasting highlights on the spindles of the chair.

1

MATERIALS
acrylic paint: deep blue
paintbrush
Rolco Quick-Dry Synthetic Gold Size Varnish
Dutch metal
scissors
Treasure Copper
water-based polyurethane
polyurethane brush

1. Prepare surface of chair (see page 26) and paint deep blue acrylic. Allow to dry, then paint second coat. Working in small areas, brush on a light but even coat of gold size varnish.

2. When varnish becomes tacky, slip on the gold leaf and smooth it down with your fingers or a soft-bristled brush.

2

3. Cut gold leaf squares into smaller pieces for easy handling when applying to spindles, rungs, and other smaller, less broad surfaces. As the edges of the leaves meet and overlap, they'll create a crackled surface texture. Highlight part of the spindles by rubbing on some Treasure Copper paste with your finger. Seal with a few coats of water-based polyurethane.

Pickling is a process of adding color (most commonly white) to a wood surface in a translucent way that leaves the grain and character of the wood visible. A thin layer of pigment penetrates the wood fibers so that the surface becomes a lighter tone. A pickled surface is a good base for any number of painting techniques — stenciling, masking, or hand painting, to name a few. But an attractive pickled piece without additional detailing or ornamentation can exude a poetic, Shaker-like clarity and simplicity that's both understated and elegant.

Pickled surfaces have been steadily gaining popularity in recent years, reflected in many commercially available wood products like oak hardwood floors and stock kitchen cabinetry. White pickled surfaces seem to be the most common, but you can lighten a wood surface with any pastel shade.

Obviously, pickling can only be done on stripped, bare wood. Any paint or sealer must be completely removed for the wood to be receptive to this treatment.

If you want to lighten up a stained piece of furniture, strip it as best you can, then wash it down with a weak bleach-and-water solution (one part bleach to four parts water), working in direct sunlight. Don't saturate the surface with the bleach solution, however, because water can raise the grain and permanently damage the wood. Remember to wear gloves and protect your eyes.

LARGE ARMOIRE

This large Virginia-made armoire with its beautiful bonnet was discovered in an antique store in North Carolina. It's a country piece with simple lines and very strong proportions. The treatment was kept simple because the piece was intended for an environment that's a little less country and a bit more formal. I had to strip off the old varnish. A second application of Woodfinisher's Pride and some steel wool enabled me to pull up and remove most of the stain as well. Instead of again staining the piece a wood tone, I've lightened and updated it by pickling it white. Detail colors are light green, dark green, and coral, applied in an opaque way that covers the wood grain. In some areas, the paint was lifted with a sponge to reveal the wood grain again.

The door panel was accented with a simplified line treatment, and the frame of the door was defined with a dark green. Dark green, light green, and coral were used to state the legs and clarify the strength of the bonnet. After a base coat of coral, the bonnet was given a very loose, freehand texture that echoes a more sophisticated veining treatment. This was done simply by twirling or rolling first an artist's brush, then a stick with black paint on it between the thumb and forefinger so it bounced against the surface, creating an irregular, spontaneous design. While still wet, these patterns were softened a bit with a moist sponge.

MATERIALS

stripping gel
interior latex paint
acrylic paint: white, light green, dark green, coral,
    black, white
flat-tipped artist's brush for pickling
sponge or rag
sandpaper
tack cloth
masking tape
tapered artist's brush
Butcher's wax

1. **Prepare surface by removing old varnish with stripping gel (see page 27 for detailed instructions). Choose a color for the inside, and give it two coats of latex.**

2. **For the pickling process, squeeze a small amount of white acrylic paint onto a plate and add a small amount of water to dilute it. Keep a bowl of water nearby to dip your flat-tipped brush in. The ratio of water to paint will determine how pale or how rich the surface tint finally becomes. Wash over the piece with the diluted paint, going with the grain of the wood. Wipe it down immediately with a sponge or rag — again following the grain of the wood — to blend and unify the surface. You can repeat this process to heighten the effect.**

    When the piece is dry, sand lightly and rub down with tack cloth. The surface must be clean and free of debris before you proceed. Accent the bonnet, legs, and door panels with the light and dark green and coral acrylic paint, using masking tape to define the inner line of the door. Allow paint to dry, then wipe down with a sponge to reveal some of the wood grain.

3. Add freehand texture using black and white paint
and both ends of an artist's brush, twirling the brush
between thumb and forefinger as described above.
When dry, finish with a coat of clear Butcher's wax.

RESOURCES

RESOURCES

Furniture and accessories in this book were obtained from the following sources.

Independent Dealers

Browsery Antiques
516 South Elm Street
Greensboro, NC 27406
(919) 274-3231

Mary Rhyne's Corner Cupboard Antiques, Inc.
603 South Elm Street
Greensboro, NC 27406
(919) 378-1380

Thumbprint Antiques
Old Tongore Road
Stone Ridge, NY 10142
(914) 331-9318

Tyler-Smith Antiques
501 Simpson Street
Greensboro, NC 27401
(919) 294-2771

Van Deusen House Antiques
11 Main Street
Hurley, NY 12443
(914) 331-8852

Chain Stores
check the yellow pages for the outlets near you
Conran's
Mastercraft
Pier 1 Imports
Wicker World

Most of the materials used in this book are widely available at hardware stores, home improvement centers, craft stores, and art supply stores. For further information about specific products, contact the following companies.

Latex paints
Benjamin Moore & Co.
51 Chestnut Ridge Road
Montvale, NJ 07645
(201) 573-9600

Butcher's wax
Butcher Polish Company
120 Bartlett Street
Marlborough, MA 01752
(508) 481-5700

Woodfinisher's Pride
both varnish and paint stripper formulas
Creative Technologies Group, Inc.
P.O. Box 669544
Charlotte, NC 28266
(800) 457-7433

Easy Mask Painting Tape
Daubert Coated Products, Inc.
1 Westbrook Corporate Center, Suite 1000
Westchester, IL 60154
(708) 409-5100

Acrylic paints
Duncan Enterprises
5673 East Shields Avenue
Fresno, CA 93727
(209) 291-4444

Varethane Diamond Finish
water-based polyurethane
Flecto Company, Inc.
Oakland, CA 94608
(510) 655-2470

Folk Art Antiquing
Plaid Enterprises, Inc.
P.O. Box 7600
Norcross, GA 30091
(404) 923-8200

Quick-Dry Synthetic Gold Size Varnish
gold leaf adhesive
Rolco Labs, Inc.
Dorset, VT 05251
(802) 867-5956

Rags-in-a-Box, drop cloth
Scott Paper Company
Scott Plaza
Philadelphia, PA 19113
(800) 835-7268

Scotch brand scrub sponges, masking tape
3M
3M Center
St. Paul, MN 55144
(800) 362-3456

PAINT RECIPES

When custom mixing colors for any project, it is a very good idea to write down your color "recipe" — either you will run out of paint before you're done with your project or you may need to touch it up in years to come.

PAINT RECIPES

PAINT RECIPES